THE MISSING BOOKS OF THE BIBLE

VOLUME I

Media Solution Services
440 Park Avenue South, 6th Floor
New York, New York 10016
Printed in Korea

CONTENTS

VOLUME I

INTRODUCTION

Have you ever heard of the warrior Judah Maccabee? If you're familiar with the story of Hanukkah, you may know of this biblical hero, who inspired an oratorio by composer George Handel and a drama by American poet Henry Wadsworth Longfellow. The story of the beautiful biblical heroine Susanna is also well-known. She was a popular subject for many famous artists, including Tintoretto, Rubens, and Rembrandt.

Yet surprisingly, their stories—as well as those of other familiar biblical characters—are missing from the English, or Protestant, version of the Bible. Why? Because they are part of the Apocrypha, a group of fifteen books that were part of the Greek translation of the Bible, but were not accepted by Protestants because they were not part of the original Hebrew Scriptures. To understand the origins of the Apocrypha, we must go back to the Bible's very beginnings.

It is important to remember that the Bible is not a single book that was composed in one place during a single period of time. Instead, it is a collection of sacred texts—histories, prophecies, prayers, philosophies, moral tales, and proverbs—that was written over many centuries by many different people. These texts were eventually accepted by Jews and, later, by Christians as Holy Scripture.

The original Jewish Holy Scriptures—the Five Books of Moses, the Prophets, and the Writings such as Psalms and Proverbs—were composed in Hebrew and Aramaic, a closely related language. This is the Bible that Jesus, as a Jew living in the Holy Land, knew and referred to in his teachings.

But long before the time of Jesus, a Greek translation of the Hebrew Bible was made in Alexandria, a city in Egypt established to honor Alexander the Great. This translation—known as the Septuagint—was familiar to the many non-Hebrew-speaking Jews who lived outside their ancestral homeland of Judah. The Septuagint was also the version that, many centuries later, spread the message of Christianity to non-Jews throughout the Roman world.

In the centuries between the original translation of the Septuagint and the rise of Christianity, however, many texts were added to the Septuagint that were never added to the Hebrew Bible. Although Jews studied and respected these additions, only the original books in the Hebrew Bible were finally accepted as sacred to Judaism.

Some time after the death of Jesus, when Christianity became a religion separate from Judaism, leaders of the new Church compiled their own Holy Scriptures. They designated the Septuagint version of the Bible—including the additions—as the Old Testament. The message of Jesus the Savior, consisting of the writings of his followers, became known as the New Testament. Together, these two documents make up today's Christian Bible.

In the fourth century, a Christian scholar named Jerome was given the task of translating the Bible into Latin. In his translation, called the Vulgate, Jerome included those books of the Old Testament which appeared in the Septuagint but not in the Hebrew Bible, as well as a few others. He proposed to call these additional books *apocrypha*.

Although this title is widely used, it frequently causes misunderstanding. At one time, *apocrypha* was a term used to describe books that were "hidden away" because they were considered too esoteric or sacred for the common reader. Later, *apocrypha* described heretical Christian works, and came to mean "questionable" or "not trustworthy." The case of the additional books of the Septuagint is different, however.

The Apocryphal books were an integral and important part of the Vulgate translation, and most remain so today in Roman Catholic Bibles. In the German translation of Martin Luther, however, they were collected into an appendix. This practice was then borrowed by the Church of England. The fact that the Old Testament and Apocrypha were now separated helps to explain why the same biblical characters are called by slightly different names in the two sections of the Bible, for example: Ezra/Esdras and Jeremiah/Jeremy. Most translations of the Old Testament are based on the Hebrew text; the Apocrypha is translated from the Greek.

At first, the Apocrypha was considered an essential part of the English Bible. In fact, one of the archbishops associated with the King James Version of 1611 issued an order forbidding the omission of the Apocrypha from Bibles. But within a few decades, many printers began to ignore this warning. By 1827, the British Bible Society had stopped including the Apocrypha in its Bibles, and the American Bible Society soon followed. Finally, the Apocrypha became the "missing" books of the Bible.

CONTENT OF THE APOCRYPHA

For a greater understanding of the history of Judaism and Christianity, these books are well worth studying. The Apocrypha illuminates Jewish thought during the years between the close of the Old Testament and the beginning of the New Testament. Many concepts that are taken for granted in the New Testament are hardly mentioned in the Old Testament, such as angels and demons, as well as reward and punishment in the afterlife. But Jesus and the apostles could assume their audiences would understand these ideas, because they figure prominently in the Apocrypha.

The Apocrypha also fills in the dramatic history of Jewish contact with Greece and Rome. When the Old Testament ends, the Land of Israel is under Persian rule. When the New Testament begins, the Romans are in control. The historical books of the Apocrypha describe some of the events between these two periods, including the Greeks' attempts to dominate the Holy Land and the arrival of the Romans. In addition, the Apocrypha gives evidence of the gradual infiltration of Greek ideas into biblical religion. The Jewish Torah, for example, became identified during this period with the Greek Wisdom, a divine force that existed even before the creation of the world. This, in turn, suggests what John the Baptist understood as Logos when he wrote, "In the beginning was the Word."

Studying the Apocrypha as a historical document presents real challenges, however. Due to one odd practice, we don't know exactly when and where the books were written, or who wrote them. Ancient authors frequently attributed their works to famous dead people in order to gain acceptance for their ideas. There is little chance, therefore, that Ezra really wrote Esdras or that Solomon actually had anything to do with writing Wisdom of Solomon.

Scholars have tried to determine the date and place of the Apocrypha's composition by studying its ideas, language, and possible references to historical events. But scholars' solutions are often controversial. Their suggested dates of composition may range over hundreds of years. They can only identify places as "probably Alexandria" or "possibly Palestine." And they may interpret an evil kingdom mentioned in a text as either Babylon, Greece, or Rome. In addition, the books themselves show many signs of insertions and other tampering. A single sentence or word inserted into a passage centuries later can change its entire meaning, and throw off all scholarly calculations. Such may be true for the other books of the Bible as well, but it's less likely. Because these books were more widely circulated, quoted, and studied, people would probably have quickly noticed changes or errors in a copy.

But these cautions should not stop readers from discovering the superb literature and wisdom of the Apocrypha. It contains wonderful short stories, beautiful poetry, clever satire and riveting history. Several works, for example, bring surprising sensitivity to their explorations of women's lives—in the stories of Susanna, Esther, and Judith.

A brief summary and discussion of each book of the Apocrypha follows.

THE FIRST BOOK OF ESDRAS

Also called the Greek Ezra and III Esdras, this book has been described as a translation, paraphrase, or retelling of the biblical Book of Ezra. Although it covers much of the same material as the Old Testament work, it contains some important differences.

For example, I Esdras opens with events that occur before the opening of Ezra, starting with the Passover festival celebrated by King Josiah as part of his religious revival. It continues with the events leading up to the destruction of the Temple in Jerusalem in 586 B.C.E.—an addition based on II Chronicles—then announces the decree of King Cyrus of Persia, which allowed the Jews to rebuild the Temple. This is the point at which the Book of Ezra begins.

A more significant addition is a contest of wits featuring Zorobabel (Zerubbabel of the Book of Ezra) in chapters 3–4. Part Eastern fairy tale, part Platonic dialogue, this story describes the competition among three of Darius's guards to name the strongest force in the world. The contest takes place before King Cyrus, who will reward the winner with the right to rebuild the Temple in Jerusalem. The first guard says wine is the strongest force, because "it causeth all men to err that drink it: It maketh the mind of the king and of the fatherless child to be all one." The second guard chooses the king, because men rule all creation, but if the king "bid them make war the one against the other, they do it. . . . They slay and are slain, and transgress not the king's commandment." The third guard, Zorobabel, proclaims that women are the strongest force in the world, because they rule even the king. Zorobabel had seen the king's lover take his crown and slap his face, "yet for all this the king gaped and gazed upon her with open mouth." After Zorobabel says this, the king and princes "looked one upon another"—perhaps amazed that Zorobabel would dare to discuss the king's intimate behavior. But Zorobabel simply adds, "great is the truth, and stronger than all things." He wins the right to rebuild the Temple.

THE SECOND BOOK OF ESDRAS

Sometimes called the Apocalypse of Ezra, this book belongs to a type of literature that prophecies the end of time. It is not found in the Septuagint, but appears in the Vulgate as IV Esdrae (the Latin form of Esdras). Martin Luther omitted it from his Bible, proclaiming its contents unworthy. The chapters of The Second Book of Ezra are sometimes subdivided: chapters 1–2 become III Esdras, chapters 3–14 become IV Esdras, and chapters 15–16 become V Esdras. This perhaps explains why the book is hard to summarize. It is a series of visions, that often appear to have little connection to each other.

Chapters 1–2 seem to be an independent work that was later added to the main text. After a long recitation of God's favors and Israel's lack of gratitude, the basic laws of morality are reviewed: "Do right to the widow, judge for the fatherless, give to the poor, defend the orphan, clothe the naked." The ultimate message is that because of Israel's sins, God will find a new chosen people for himself.

In three visions in chapters 3–9, Ezra laments the destruction of Zion and the suffering of the righteous. The angel Uriel tells him that man cannot understand God's ways. Ezra responds that it would be better not to have been created than to suffer without knowing why. He is told that evil will rule for only a limited time, and then the righteous will enjoy resurrection. Ezra asks when this will happen, for "what is past I know, but what is for to come I know not." The angel answers that, just as a few drops remain after the rain passes, only a little time remains before the resurrection. Ezra complains that Israel has suffered too much. He is again assured of the resurrection. Now, however, he is saddened by the small number who will be saved. The angel replies that just as a planter sows many seeds but few take root, so too all who are sown in the world are not saved. Then the angel assures Ezra, "Unto you is paradise opened."

In the next chapter, Ezra sees a woman mourning her dead son. He asks how she can mourn for one child when Jerusalem and so many of its inhabitants have perished, and tells her to accept God's decree: "Now therefore keep thy sorrow to thyself, and bear with a good courage that which hath befallen thee." For if she does this, Ezra claims, she will see her son again in due time. The woman becomes a blindingly bright vision and disappears. A large city appears in her place. The angel explains that the woman is Zion, and those who mourn her will see her glory again.

In chapters 11–12, Ezra has a vision of an eagle emerging from the sea; it has twelve wings and three heads and rules the world. Finally, it is driven away by a lion. The angel tells Ezra that the eagle is the fourth kingdom (usually understood to be Rome) predicted by Daniel, and the lion is the Messiah, from the seed of David. In the next chapter, Ezra sees a man, in fact the Messiah, who is attacked from all sides. The man overcomes his attackers with words rather than weapons.

Chapter 14 contains what is called the Ezra Legend. Ezra is commanded to write holy books, to set his house in order, and to forgo the cares of mortality: "For the world has lost his youth, and the times begin to wax old." Ezra asks how he will know what to write, and is told, "I shall light a candle of understanding in thine heart, which shall not be put out." With the help of five men, Ezra writes ninety-four books. Twenty-four are made public; seventy are hidden. Since the Hebrew Bible contains twenty-four books, this vision is usually interpreted as a defense of the hidden books—the apocryphal writings that are not in the Bible.

The final two chapters foretell the destruction of Babylon, Asia, Egypt, and Syria. This section is different from the preceding visions in both form and content. Most scholars believe that it was originally a separate work.

THE BOOK OF TOBIT

Until the nineteenth century, the story of Tobit was among the most popular in Western literature—a timeless tale of love and loyalty, religion and morality, with many charming touches. It was copied and recopied, translated into numerous languages, and explored in paintings by the greatest names in art. Martin Luther said of it, "Is it history? Then it is holy history. Is it fiction? Then it is truly beautiful, wholesome and profitable fiction."

Tobit is a righteous man, honest in business, compassionate to the poor. Although he lives in exile, he is careful to follow the religious rituals of his homeland: "[W]hen we were carried away captives to Nineveh, all my brethren . . . did eat of the bread of the Gentiles. But I kept myself from eating; because I remembered God with all my heart." Tobit is particularly dedicated to honoring the many martyrs who have died for their faith. He seeks out their corpses, which have been "cast about the walls" and "cast out in the marketplace," and in defiance of the government, secretly buries them. On one occasion, he is resting after such a burial and is blinded when bird droppings fall into his eyes. Reduced to poverty, he is taunted by his wife, who asks, "Where are thine alms and thy righteous deeds?" But he prays to God for justice and mercy.

Meanwhile, in Ecbatana, Sarah, the daughter of Tobit's relative, has just lost her seventh husband to the demon Asmodeus, who has killed each of Sarah's husbands on their wedding night. Unable to stand the reproach of her neighbors, Sarah asks God to kill her, or at least, "if it please not thee that I should die, command some regard to be had of me, and pity taken of me, that I hear no more reproach." God sends the angel Raphael in disguise to help Tobit and Sarah.

Tobit remembers that someone in Ragae owes him money, and sends his son Tobias to collect it. Before Tobias leaves, Tobit urges him to live a moral and religious life: "My son, when I am dead, bury me; and despise not your mother, but honor her all the days of thy life. . . . If thou hast abundance, give alms accordingly: if thou have but little, be not afraid to give according to that little." In an especially important passage, Tobit reminds Tobias of the Golden Rule: "Do that to no man which thou hatest." Tobias hires a guide—the disguised Raphael—and "they went forth both, and the young man's dog with them."

The dog is an unusual touch. Pets are common today, but they are a rarity in the Bible and early religious literature. Tobias's dog plays no part in the drama of the story—it does not kill the demon or find the missing money. It is present simply as Tobias's pet.

At the Tigris River, Raphael tells Tobias to catch a certain fish and take its heart, liver, and gall. In Ecbatana, Raphael arranges for Tobias to marry his cousin Sarah, because "according to the law of Moses . . . the right of inheritance doth rather appertain to thee." That is, a childless widow must marry her kinsman, although in Deuteronomy 25:5-10 and Ruth 3 a woman marries her husband's kinsman, not her own. In the bridal chamber, Tobias destroys Asmodeus with the heart and liver of the fish. Then Tobias and Sarah pray: "Blessed art thou, O God of our fathers . . . Thou madest Adam, and gavest him Eve his wife for an helper and stay. . . . And now, O Lord, I take not this my sister for lust, but uprightly: therefore mercifully ordain that we may become aged together."

During the two-week wedding feast, Raphael goes to Ragae to collect Tobit's money. Afterward, Raphael, Tobias, and Sarah start back to Tobit. Tobias carries the gall of the fish, "and the dog went after them." In Nineveh, Tobias cures Tobit with the gall. Raphael reveals himself as "one of the seven holy angels, which present the prayers" and expounds on the merit of good deeds: "It is better to give alms than to lay up gold: For alms doth deliver from death."

As in the last passage, the book is filled with echoes from other books of the Bible. This suggests the ways in which early biblical law shaped daily life, and the way biblical quotations were already incorporated into private prayer.

THE BOOK OF JUDITH

Like the story of Tobit, the Book of Judith stresses the importance of religious observance. Unlike Tobit, it has the suspenseful plot of a thriller.

Holofernes, commander of the Assyrian army, besieges the Jewish city of Bethulia. An ally tells him, however, that war is futile: "[I]f there be any error in this people, and they sin against their God . . . we shall overcome them. But if there be no iniquity in their nation, let my lord now pass by, lest their Lord defend them." Holofernes rejects this advice and prepares for war. He cuts off the water supply to the city. In Bethulia, "women and young men fainted for thirst, and fell down in the streets."

At the insistence of the citizens, the elders decide that if God does not save them in five days, they will surrender the city. But Judith, a beautiful young widow, chides them: "Do not bind the counsels of the Lord our God: for God is not as man, that he may be threatened." Rather, she says, since the whole nation has abandoned idolatry—the cause of earlier punishment—"therefore we trust that he will not despise us."

Judith devises a plan and prays that she should be the vehicle of her people's salvation: "Smite by the deceit of my lips the servant with the prince, and the prince with the servant: break down their stateliness by the hand of a woman." And, in a passage that distinguishes the Judeo-Christian God from all the ancient gods of kings and warriors, she continues: "For . . . thou art a God of the afflicted, an helper of the oppressed, an upholder of the weak, a protector of the forlorn, a savior of them that are without hope." She then dresses in her finest clothes—"her garments of gladness"—and leaves the city for the Assyrian camp.

When Judith tells the guards that she will show them how to capture the city without a fight, they take her to Holofernes. She advises him that the only way to defeat the Jews is to wait for them to sin against

God; being a religious woman, she will know when this happens. All she asks is that each night she be allowed to go outside the camp to pray; God will inform her of the time, and she will inform Holofernes. Everyone marvels at her "beauty of face, and wisdom of words."

For three days she prays, refusing to eat forbidden food. On the fourth day, Holofernes insists that she dine alone with him in his tent. He confides to a servant, "For, lo, it will be a shame for our person, if we shall let such a woman go, not having had her company; for if we draw her not unto us, she will laugh us to scorn." Judith accepts, saying to the servant that "whatsoever pleaseth him I will do speedily, and it shall be my joy."

Holofernes is so excited that he drinks "much more wine than he had drunk at any time in one day since he was born." On cue, all the servants leave. But Holofernes passes out. Judith finds his sword and cuts off his head. She puts it into her bag, tells the guard she is going outside the camp to pray, and returns safely to Bethulia, where she is honored as the savior of her people.

Many modern critics claim offense that this story is part of Holy Scripture. They disapprove of the exultation over the death of Holofernes. Some have even called Judith a murderer. However, this story is typical of the entire Book of Judges and much of Samuel and Kings.

The plot is similar to many popular stories and movies in which the law-abiding hero saves the day with an uncharacteristic act of violence. On a literal level, it shows how a woman's sexual vulnerability can become a source of strength. Early Church teachers saw Judith as symbolic of the victory of the Virgin over the Devil, or of Chastity over Lust.

THE REST OF THE CHAPTERS OF THE BOOK OF ESTHER

The Septuagint version of the Book of Esther contains several significant additions missing from the Hebrew text. Jerome placed these additions at the end of the Vulgate as separate chapters. In English Bibles, these new chapters are placed in the Apocrypha. They are therefore difficult to follow in their present form. The best way to read them is to insert them back into the Old Testament Esther.

The story of Esther is a carefully crafted drama of plots and counterplots, filled with wit and irony. In a drunken rage, the Persian King (Ahasuerus in Hebrew, Artaxerxes in Greek) banishes his queen and holds a contest to choose a new favorite. Esther, the orphaned ward of a Jew named Mordecai (Mardochaeus), wins the contest and becomes queen, but keeps her religion a secret. Without revealing his connection to Esther, Mordecai foils a plot to kill the king. Haman, a powerful courtier, takes a dislike to Mordecai. Feeling that it is beneath his dignity to kill only Mordecai, Haman gets permission to destroy the entire Jewish community. A day is set and a decree is issued to sanction the slaughter. Mordecai tells Esther that divine providence must have put her on the throne: she alone can save the Jews. At dinner with the king and Haman, she reveals her religion and accuses Haman of trying to kill her. Astonished—and perhaps drunk—the king rushes out of the room for air. Haman throws himself across Esther's seat and begs for mercy. The king returns and accuses Haman of trying to rape Esther. Haman is executed, but it is too late to rescind the decree. The Jews are given permission to defend themselves, and many royal officials help them fight off their attackers.

It is worth noting that the English translation of this story, which in the original uses language so carefully, misleads many readers. The original decree (3:12ff.) allows Haman's army "to destroy, to kill, and cause to perish, all Jews, both young and old, little children and women . . . and to take the spoil." The letter permitting the Jews to defend themselves (8:9ff.) says that "the king granted the Jews . . . to stand for their life, to destroy, to slay, and to cause to perish, all the power of the people and province that would assault them, both little ones and women, and to take the spoil." This has been interpreted to mean that the Jews slaughtered the families of their enemies. But, more likely, it is an ironic echo of the original decree. The ones whom they are permitted to kill are those who tried to assault "them, both little ones and women, and to take the spoil." This interpretation is supported by the later statement that the Jews did not take spoil but merely stood in self-defense, something they could not have done if the power of the government were still behind Haman's forces.

Where do the "Rest of the Chapters of Esther" fit into this story?

The first sentence of chapter 11 is the last sentence of the Greek version. It identifies the translator. The rest of the chapter is the prologue in the Greek version. It describes the dream of Mardochaeus, in which two dragons fight and frighten the whole world, a small stream becomes a mighty river, and the humble are raised up. Mardochaeus awakens and ponders the meaning of the dream.

Chapter 10 is the epilogue, and explains how the story of Mardochaeus, Esther, and Haman was predicted by the dream. The two dragons are Mardochaeus and Haman. Esther is the stream that became a river.

Chapter 12 of these additions to the Apocrypha repeats the last scene of chapter 2 of the Old Testament version, with two important differences. First, Esther is not the one who delivers Mardochaeus's message. Second, Haman vows vengeance on Mardochaeus because of the death of the conspirators.

The first part of chapter 13 of the Apocrypha belongs after verse 3:13 of the Old Testament Esther. It is the text of the decree ordering the destruction of the Jews. In effect it repeats Haman's charge that the Jews follow their own laws, and it adds the charge that they are hostile to all other people and disloyal to the king.

The second part of the chapter is the prayer of Mardochaeus after he has urged Esther to intercede with the king. Since the immediate cause of Haman's anger was Mardochaeus's refusal to bow down to him, Mardochaeus assures God that this refusal was not because of personal pride but because he could not give a man the honor due only to God. This section stands after verse 4:17 of the Old Testament text.

Chapter 14, which immediately follows the previous passage, is Esther's prayer before she visits the king without a summons—a capital crime. She acknowledges that sin has brought exile and the loss of national sovereignty to the Jews, but argues that her people do not deserve total destruction. She also states that she hates being queen—sharing the bed of a Gentile and facing the temptation of forbidden food and wine. This lament gives force to Mardochaeus's argument that she should use her position to save the Jews. As she obviously does not enjoy being queen, her position is clearly not her reward for good deeds; it must be part of God's hidden plan.

Chapter 15 provides an introduction to chapter 5 of the Hebrew Book of Esther. Esther adorns herself and goes to the throne-room. Overcome with fear, she faints. The king is moved to pity and assures her that she is safe.

Chapter 16 contains the text of the edict permitting the Jews to defend themselves. The edict declares that, far from being disloyal and hostile, the Jews are a moral, peace-loving people. As for the previous decree, the edict explains that it was the work of people who misuse their office and take advantage of the king's goodwill. Significantly, this passage calls Haman a Macedonian and explains that the destruction of the Jews was part of a larger plot to weaken Persia so that the Greeks could conquer her. Scholars use this passage as proof that the additions were written during a period of resistance to Hellenism (adopting Greek beliefs), either under the Hasmoneans or later.

In general, the visions and prayers of the Apocrypha chapters give this version of Esther an explicit religious message, in contrast to the Hebrew text, where the hand of God, if present at all, is hidden in human actions.

THE WISDOM OF SOLOMON

This is a major philosophical work, in which a traditional Jew confronts and adapts Hellenistic thought.

The book falls into three parts: The first is a discussion of "last things," such as the afterlife; the second a hymn to Wisdom; and the third an explanation of the Exodus in terms of "measure for measure."

The Wisdom of Solomon contains, among many other important ideas, a major statement supporting the immortality of the soul: "God created man to be immortal, and made him to be an image of his own eternity" (2:23).

This book also contains this description of reward and punishment in the afterlife: "The souls of the righteous are in the hand of God, and there shall no torment touch them. In the sight of the unwise they seemed to die: and their departure is taken for misery. And their going from us to be utter destruction: but they are in peace" (3:1-3).

The work is composed in poetically balanced lines; the argument is clear and flows with a logical, compelling force. For example, chapter 2 explains that evil, or sin, results from a belief that consciousness ends with death of the body. Projecting himself into the minds of evildoers, the author lets us experience their reasoning, which begins with the idea that a person should seize the day and enjoy life:

"For the ungodly said, reasoning with themselves, but not aright, Our life is short and tedious, and in the death of a man there is no remedy. . . . our body shall be turned into ashes, and our spirit shall vanish as the soft air. . . . Come on therefore, let us enjoy the good things that are present. . . ." (2:1-6).

This reasoning soon leads to ignoring right and wrong: "Let none of us go without his part of our voluptuousness . . . for this is our portion, and our lot is this. Let us oppress the poor righteous man, let us not spare the widow, nor reverence the ancient gray hairs of the aged" (2:9-10). Such thoughts inevitably justify blasphemy and gratuitous evil:

"Let us see if his words be true: and let us prove

what shall happen in the end of him. For if the just man be the son of God, he will help him, and deliver him from the hand of his enemies. Let us examine him with despitefulness and torture, that we may know his meekness, and prove his patience" (2:17-19).

The author returns to his own voice, and comments: "Such things they did imagine, and were deceived: for their own wickedness hath blinded them" (2:21).

The hymn to Wisdom identifies her as "the breath of the power of God, and a pure influence flowing from the glory of the Almighty" (7:25). And, apparently borrowing from Greek thought, it credits Wisdom with being the source of "temperance and prudence, justice and fortitude" (8:7). So, too, it connects a biblical idea, that humans cannot fathom God, to the Platonic explanation (later used by Paul in I Corinthians 15:54 and II Corinthians 5:1) that "the corruptible body presseth down the soul, and the earthly tabernacle weigheth down the mind" (9:15).

The final section, in its review of Jewish history, includes a satire on idolatry similar to one found in the Apocryphal Epistle of Jeremy: "For health [the idolater] calleth upon that which is weak: for life prayeth to that which is dead" (13:18). But here the author also adds that this idolatry is performed with deliberate disregard for pride and logic: "Now a carpenter . . . taking the very refuse among those which served to no use . . . when he had nothing else to do . . . fashioned it to the image of a man . . . and is not ashamed to speak to that which hath no life" (13:11-17). It must follow, the author concludes, that such a people will naturally turn to antisocial behavior: "They kept neither lives nor marriages any longer undefiled. . . . For the worshiping of idols not to be named is the beginning, the cause, and the end, of all evil" (14:24-27).

THE WISDOM OF JESUS THE SON OF SIRACH

Also called The Wisdom of Ben Sira (Hebrew for son of Sira), this was perhaps the most widely regarded book of the Apocrypha. Its extensive use in church liturgy gave rise to its alternative name, Ecclesiaticus, not to be confused with the Old Testament book Ecclesiastes.

The author, a Palestinian Jew, is called Yeshua (Joshua) Ben Sira in Hebrew, rendered in Greek as Jesus, the son of Sirach. Since evidence in the text suggests that he was a younger contemporary of the High Priest Simon, son of Onias (see chapter 50), who died in 196 B.C.E., Yeshua probably wrote between 190–180 B.C.E. The Greek translation was made by his grandson some fifty years later.

Like the Old Testament Book of Proverbs, most of this book is a collection of maxims, usually grouped by topic, about public morality and private behavior. Chapters 44–50, which begin, "Let us now praise famous men," honor Israel's heroes. Chapter 51 contains a prayer of thanksgiving and a hymn to wisdom.

Unlike most ancient collections of proverbs, this book is addressed not to rulers, but to the average head of a family. He is counseled on dealings with his wife and children and the treatment of friends, as well as on other practical matters. The three things that make a person "beautiful before God and men" are "the unity of brethren, the love of neighbors, a man and a wife that agree together" (25:1).

Notably, the author of The Wisdom of Jesus the Son of Sirach does not claim divine guidance for his work. He says merely that he has studied and wants to share what he has learned: "I awaked up last of all, as one that gathereth after the grapegatherers . . . and filled my winepress like a gatherer of grapes" (33:16). In addition, he explicitly rejects the notion of an afterlife: "Thanksgiving perisheth from the dead, as from one that is not: . . . the son of man is not immortal" (17:28-30).

Nevertheless, he views religion as the basis of a meaningful life: "To fear the Lord is the beginning of wisdom" (1:14). "All wisdom cometh from the Lord" (1:1), but man is limited, "for more things are showed unto thee than men understand. For many are deceived by their own vain opinion" (3:23-24). Therefore, a man should honor and help his parents, be humble and honest in business, "defraud not the poor of his living. . . . Add not more trouble to an heart that is vexed. . . . Reject not the supplication of the afflicted" (4:1-4). In contrast, "The beginning of pride is when one departeth from God. . . . For pride is the beginning of sin" (10:12-13).

Many quotable lines are found in this work:

> A faithful friend is a strong defence, and he that hath found such an one hath found a treasure (6:14).
>
> Rejoice not over thy greatest enemy being dead, but remember that we die all (8:7).
>
> Open not thine heart to every man (8:19).
>
> The heart of fools is in their mouth: but the mouth of the wise is in their heart (21:26).

THE BOOK OF BARUCH

Baruch is the scribe who recorded the prophet Jeremiah's speeches. For this reason, several early Church Fathers quoted passages from this book as the words of Jeremiah. They considered verse 3:37 especially significant because it could be taken as a foretelling of Jesus: "Afterwards did he show himself upon earth, and conversed with men."

The book falls into three sections. The first part, in prose, includes a historical setting like the one found in Daniel 9, as well as a similar confession and prayer: suffering is punishment for sin, but God is just and merciful; may God look down from heaven and save us.

Most of chapter 3 is a poem in praise of Wisdom, here equated with the Torah, or Law. Wisdom is not the possession of the rich and powerful, nor that of Canaan and the children of the East. Only God is all-knowing, and he has given this gift of wisdom to Israel, as a way of life. Rather than seeking knowledge elsewhere, the children of Israel should return to the source of their glory.

The last section offers two poetic laments. In most of chapter 4, a personified Jerusalem consoles Israel, as a mother cares for her children. In the remainder of the book, the poet consoles Jerusalem with assurances of redemption.

THE EPISTLE OF JEREMY

Sometimes appended to the Book of Baruch as chapter 6, this short work is a satire on idolatry similar to the one found in Wisdom of Solomon. The author tells the exiled Jews that they should neither fear nor worship the gods of their conquerors, for idols have no more power than "a scarecrow in a garden of cucumbers."

Each section ends with a variation of the refrain "They are not Gods."

The Epistle of Jeremy seems to be an elaboration of Jeremiah 10:2-5:

"Thus saith the Lord, Learn not the way of the heathen, and be not dismayed at the signs of heaven; for the heathen are dismayed at them. For the customs of the people are vain: for one cutteth a tree out of the forest, the work of the hands of the workman, with the axe. They deck it with silver and with gold; they fasten it with nails and with hammers, that it move not. They are upright as the palm tree, but speak not: they must needs be borne, because they cannot go. Be not afraid of them; for they cannot do evil, neither also is it in them to do good."

In the same vein, the Epistle says that heathens ask their idols for help, but the idols cannot even help themselves. Sometimes their priests steal their gold and silver ornaments. If they fall, they cannot get up. If there is a fire, someone must carry them to safety. Their temples must be locked so that they are not stolen. Birds perch on their heads, and insects eat their clothes. How can anyone fear such gods?

The author also notes that idol worship is immoral. It does not lead to pity for the widow or orphan, nor aid to the needy. Rather, it fosters temple prostitution and jealousy. It brings only disgrace to its followers.

THE PRAYER OF AZARIAH

This short text is not a separate book, but an addition to the Book of Daniel.

Azariah is the Hebrew name of Abednego, the friend of Daniel, who, along with Shadrach and Meshach (Hananiah and Mishael in Hebrew), was thrown into the fiery furnace. This prayer and the accompanying Song of the Three Children are an insertion between verses 3:23 and 24 of Daniel.

The Prayer praises God, acknowledges Israel's sin and God's justice, and pleads for mercy and deliverance. The last line (verse 22) is notable: it is a wish that all the nations of the world will recognize the one God.

The Song is a call for all creation—heavenly bodies, forces of nature, living creatures—to worship the one true God. It is similar to, and perhaps modeled on, Psalms 136 and 148.

The content echoes Psalm 148, which begins:

> Praise ye the Lord. Praise ye the Lord from the heavens: praise him in the heights.
> Praise ye him, all his angels: praise ye him, all his hosts.
> Praise ye him, sun and moon: praise him, all ye stars of light.

The choral structure is similar to that of Psalm 136:

> O give thanks unto the Lord; for he is good:
> for his mercy endureth forever.
> O give thanks unto the God of God:
> for his mercy endureth forever.
> O give thanks to the Lord of lords:
> for his mercy endureth forever.

If we imagine the Psalms as they were sung during public worship, in the Temple in Jerusalem, for example, we can readily picture a choir responding to a leader, or pilgrims repeating a refrain after each verse chanted by the choir. We might speculate that the Song of the Three Children is a similar type of psalm.

THE HISTORY OF SUSANNA

This short tale describes how a chaste woman, falsely accused of adultery and condemned to death, is saved at the last moment by a clever youth. Two corrupt elders see Susanna, a beautiful married woman, bathing in her garden, and are filled with lust. When she rejects their advances, they publicly testify that they caught her in an adulterous affair. As she is led away to be executed, Daniel asks permission to cross-examine the witnesses and catches them in a contradiction. Susanna is saved and Daniel is hailed for his brilliance.

Though it now stands alone, this story seems to have been originally intended as a prologue to the Book of Daniel, since it introduces Daniel as a youth who shows intellectual promise. Shakespeare referred to this aspect of the story in his use of the phrase "a Daniel come to judgement." Because the Old Testament Daniel is not a judge, Shakespeare must have learned the story of Susanna from the Apocrypha.

Medieval Christian commentators interpreted the focus on sexuality in the book either as an allegory, with Susanna as the persecuted church and her husband as Christ, or as a moral tale that demonstrated the triumph of virtue. Interestingly, the bathing scene was very popular among Bible illustrators and humanist painters of the sixteenth and seventeenth centuries, perhaps because it offered an excuse to paint a beautiful naked woman.

On another level, the story is strikingly modern, as it illustrates the plight of a woman in a male-dominated world. If Susanna submits to the elders, she will be committing a capital offense. But if she resists, the elders will accuse her of adultery. She understands that their word will be accepted over hers: "I am straitened on every side: for if I do this thing, it is death unto me: and if I do it not, I cannot escape your hands." As she predicts, the community believes the false testimony. Even her vindication does not come about because the judges believe her. She is saved only when they agree to hear a young man, Daniel, who finds a flaw in the elders' testimony.

THE HISTORY OF THE DESTRUCTION OF BEL AND THE DRAGON

These two vignettes were also added to the Book of Daniel, and, like the story of Susanna, they illustrate Daniel's cleverness.

Both stories reveal the foolishness of idolatry. In the first, Daniel proves to the Persian king that the idol Bel does not eat the food left for him. After offerings to Bel are placed in the temple and everyone else has left, Daniel sprinkles ashes on the floor. In the morning, he shows the king the footprints of the priests who crept in during the night to take the food.

In the second episode, Daniel kills a sacred snake by feeding it pitch, fat, and hair. The Babylonians are furious, and Daniel is thrown into the lion-pit. Hundreds of miles away in Judea, the prophet Habakkuk is making a stew. An angel grabs him by the hair and flies him to Babylon to feed Daniel. The king is very impressed, and praises Daniel's God above all others.

THE PRAYER OF MANASSES

According to II Kings 21, Manasseh "did that which was evil in the sight of the Lord" throughout his long reign: he built altars to Baal, worshiped the host of heaven, desecrated the Temple, and "shed innocent blood very much." But II Chronicles 33:11-25 says that he repented, prayed for forgiveness, and tried to undo the damage he had caused. Moreover, "his prayer unto his God . . . [is] written in the book of the kings of Israel . . . [and] among the sayings of the seers." This brief poem in the Apocrypha is believed to be that prayer.

The two central themes of the poem are that God's mercy is boundless and that God accepts true repentance. The poem even contains the bold assertion (verses 7-8) that God created repentance for the sake of the wicked, because the righteous do not need it.

THE FIRST BOOK OF MACCABEES

This book is a fairly objective account of the Jewish war of liberation against the overlords of Israel (also called Judah) in 175-135 B.C.E. It incorporates what seem to be official documents from several royal archives. The title of the book comes from its central character, Judah Maccabee (Judas Maccabeus), who gave his name to the army he led. His surname is usually taken to mean "hammer," referring to his military prowess.

The book begins with the conquests of Alexander the Great and the division of his kingdom among his generals. The land of Israel falls to Antiochus of Syria, who bans Jewish rituals and festivals. Thereafter, many of the Jews find Greek culture attractive and gladly accept assimilation. But the priest Mattathias cries out, "Whosoever is zealous of the law . . . let him follow me." He and his five sons lead a rebellion. Judah emerges as a mighty warrior and guerrilla strategist. His army captures the Temple in Jerusalem and besieges the remaining Greek garrison. The Temple is rededicated, and the festival of Hanukkah is established. The Jews are granted religious liberty, but the war against the Greeks and those who conformed to Greek beliefs continues. Judah and two of his brothers fall in battle. Jonathan assumes leadership, expands the area controlled by the Maccabees, and negotiates with various foreign powers. But he is treacherously murdered. Simon, the last surviving brother, finally wins independence. He is named High Priest and Governor. Upon his assassination, his son John becomes High Priest, and later King.

The major source of knowledge about this period of Jewish history, the First Book of Maccabees also offers a number of insights into religious practices of the time. For example, loyalty to the Sabbath was so great that a thousand Jews chose to die rather than fight their attackers on that day. Mattathias decrees, "Whosoever shall come to make battle with us on the sabbath day, we will fight against him" (2:34-42). Also, in accordance with Deuteronomy 20, Judah exempts from battle all those soldiers who have recently married, built new homes, or are afraid (3:56). Finally, the author avoids using the Tetragrammaton (God's name in Hebrew), preferring euphemisms like "heaven."

THE SECOND BOOK OF MACCABEES

Despite the title, the Second Book of Maccabees is not a continuation of The First Book of Maccabees. It is a partial summary of a much longer work, covering only the first fifteen years of I Maccabees. Rather than a factual history, it more closely resembles a morality tale, where angels interact with humans, and many scenes of martyrdom are portrayed.

One of its most moving stories is that of Eleazar (chapter 6), an aged scribe, who is forced to eat swine's flesh in public. When he refuses, his tormentors tell him he can eat whatever he wishes, as long as he appears to be eating the forbidden food. Again he refuses, because "through mine hypocrisy, and desire to live a little time and a moment longer," people will be misled. With his dying breath he proclaims that God knows "I might have been delivered from death . . . but in soul am well content to suffer these things, because I fear him."

Another story of martyrdom (chapter 7) describes a woman who sees six of her seven children tortured and killed for refusing to eat swine. When the seventh is to be killed, the king asks the mother to save her child by persuading him to submit. Instead, she says, "O my son, have pity upon me that bare thee nine months in my womb. . . . Fear not this tormentor, but, being worthy of thy brethren, take thy death."

—Harvey Minkoff, Ph.D.

Harvey Minkoff, Ph.D., is Professor of English Linguistics at Hunter College of the City University of New York. A Bible scholar who knows Hebrew, Latin, and several other languages, he has published many articles about the language and literary structure of the Bible. Most recently he edited a two-volume work entitled *Approaches to the Bible*.

THE FIRST BOOK OF ESDRAS

1 [1] And Josias held the feast of the passover in Jerusalem unto his Lord, and offered the passover the fourteenth day of the first month; [2] having set the priests according to their daily courses, being arrayed in long garments, in the temple of the Lord. [3] And he spake unto the Levites, the holy ministers of Israel, that they should hallow themselves unto the Lord, to set the holy ark of the Lord in the house that king Solomon the son of David had built: [4] and said, Ye shall no more bear the ark upon your shoulders: now therefore serve the Lord your God, and minister unto his people Israel, and prepare you after your families and kindreds, [5] according as David the king of Israel prescribed, and according to the magnificence of Solomon his son: and standing in the temple according to the several dignities of the families of you the Levites, who minister in the presence of your brethren the children of Israel, [6] offer the passover in order, and make ready the sacrifices for your brethren, and keep the passover according to the commandment of the Lord, which was given unto Moses. [7] And unto the people that was found there Josias gave

thirty thousand lambs and kids, and three thousand calves: these things were given of the king's allowance, according as he promised, to the people, to the priests, and to the Levites. [8] And Helkias, Zacharias, and Syelus, the governors of the temple, gave to the priests for the passover two thousand and six hundred sheep, and three hundred calves. [9] And Jeconias, and Samaias, and Nathanael his brother, and Assabias, and Ochiel, and Joram, captains over thousands, gave to the Levites for the passover five thousand sheep, and seven hundred calves. [10] And when these things were done, the priests and Levites, having the unleavened bread, stood in very comely order according to the kindreds, [11] and according to the several dignities of the fathers, before the people, to offer to the Lord, as it is written in the book of Moses: and thus did they in the morning. [12] And they roasted the passover with fire, as appertaineth: as for the sacrifices, they sod them in brass pots and pans with a good savour, [13] and set them before all the people: and afterward they prepared for themselves, and for the priests their brethren, the sons of Aaron. [14] For the priests offered the fat until night: and the Levites prepared for themselves, and the priests their brethren, the sons of Aaron. [15] The holy singers also, the sons of Asaph, were in their order, according to the appointment of David, to wit, Asaph, Zacharias, and Jeduthun, who was of the king's retinue. [16] Moreover the porters were at every gate; it was not lawful for any to go from his ordinary service: for their brethren the Levites prepared for them. [17] Thus were the things that belonged to the sacrifices of the Lord accomplished in that day, that they might hold the passover, [18] and offer sacrifices upon the altar of the Lord, according to the commandment of king Josias. [19] So the children of

Israel which were present held the passover at that time, and the feast of sweet bread seven days. [20] And such a passover was not kept in Israel since the time of the prophet Samuel. [21] Yea, all the kings of Israel held not such a passover as Josias, and the priests, and the Levites, and the Jews, held with all Israel that were found dwelling at Jerusalem. [22] In the eighteenth year of the reign of Josias was this passover kept. [23] And the works of Josias were upright before his Lord with an heart full of godliness. [24] As for the things that came to pass in his time, they were written in former times, concerning those that sinned, and did wickedly against the Lord above all people and kingdoms, and how they grieved him exceedingly, so that the words of the Lord rose up against Israel. [25] Now after all these acts of Josias it came to pass, that Pharaoh the king of Egypt came to raise war at Carchamis upon Euphrates: and Josias went out against him. [26] But the king of Egypt sent to him, saying, What have I to do with thee, O king of Judea? [27] I am not sent out from the Lord God against thee; for my war is upon Euphrates: and now the Lord is with me, yea, the Lord is with me hasting me forward: depart from me, and be not against the Lord. [28] Howbeit Josias did not turn back his chariot from him, but undertook to fight with him, not regarding the words of the prophet Jeremy spoken by the mouth of the Lord: [29] but joined battle with him in the plain of Magiddo, and the princes came against king Josias. [30] Then said the king unto his servants, Carry me away out of the battle; for I am very weak. And immediately his servants took him away out of the battle. [31] Then gat he up upon his second chariot; and being brought back to Jerusalem died, and was buried in his father's sepulchre. [32] And in all Jewry they mourned for Josias, yea, Jeremy the prophet lamented for Josias, and the chief men with the women made lamentation for him unto this day: and this was given out for an ordinance to be done continually in all the nation of Israel. [33] These things are written in the book of the stories of the kings of Judah, and every one of the acts that Josias did, and his glory, and his understanding in the law of the Lord, and the things that he had done before, and the things now recited, are reported in the book of the kings of Israel and Judea. [34] And the people took Joachaz the son of Josias, and made him king instead of Josias his father, when he was twenty and three years old. [35] And he reigned in Judea and in Jerusalem three months: and then the king of Egypt deposed him from reigning in Jerusalem. [36] And he set a tax upon the land of an hundred talents of silver and one talent of gold. [37] The king of Egypt also made king Joacim his brother king of Judea and Jerusalem. [38] And he bound Joacim and the nobles: but Zaraces his brother he apprehended, and brought him out of Egypt. [39] Five and twenty years old was Joacim when he was made king in the land of Judea and Jerusalem; and he did evil before the Lord. [40] Wherefore against him Nabuchodonosor the king of Babylon came up, and bound him with a chain of brass, and carried him into Babylon. [41] Nabuchodonosor also took of the holy vessels of the Lord, and carried them away, and set them in his own temple at Babylon. [42] But those things that are recorded of him, and of his uncleanliness and impiety, are written in the chronicles of the kings. [43] And Joacim his son reigned in his stead: he was made king being eighteen years old; [44] and reigned but three months and ten days in Jerusalem; and did evil before the Lord. [45] So after a year Nabuchodonosor sent and caused him to be brought into Babylon with the holy vessels of the Lord; [46] and made Zedechias king of Judea and Jerusalem, when he was one and twenty years old; and he reigned eleven years: [47] And he did evil also in the sight of the Lord, and cared not for the words that were spoken unto him by the prophet Jeremy from the mouth of the Lord. [48] And after that king Nabuchodonosor had made him to swear by the name of the Lord, he forswore himself, and rebelled; and hardening his neck and his heart, he transgressed the laws of the Lord God of Israel. [49] The governors also of the people and of the priests did many things against the laws, and passed all the pollutions of all nations, and defiled the temple of the Lord, which was sanctified in Jerusalem. [50] Nevertheless the God of their fathers sent by his messenger to call them back, because he spared them and his tabernacle also. [51] But they had his messengers in derision; and, look, when the Lord spake unto them, they made a sport of his prophets: [52] So far forth, that he, being wroth with his people for their great ungodliness, commanded the kings of the Chaldees to come up against them; [53] who slew their young men with the sword, yea, even within the compass of their holy temple, and spared neither young man nor maid, old man nor child, among them; for he delivered all into their hands. [54] And they took all the holy vessels of the Lord, both great and small, with the vessels of the ark of God, and the king's treasures, and carried them away into Babylon. [55] As for the house of the Lord, they burnt it, and brake down the walls of Jerusalem, and set fire upon her towers: [56] And as for her glorious things, they never ceased till they had consumed and brought them all to nought: and the people that were not slain with the sword he carried unto Babylon: [57] who became servants to him and his children, till the Persians reigned, to fulfil the word of the Lord spoken by the mouth of Jeremy: [58] Until the land had enjoyed her sabbaths, the whole time of her desolation shall she rest, until the full term of seventy years.

2 [1] In the first year of Cyrus king of the Persians, that the word of the Lord might be accomplished, that he had promised by the mouth of Jeremy; [2] the Lord raised up the spirit of Cyrus the king of the Persians, and he made proclamation through all his kingdom, and also by writing, [3] saying, Thus saith Cyrus king of the Persians; The Lord of Israel, the most high Lord, hath made me king of the whole world, [4] and commanded me to build him an house at Jerusalem in Jewry. [5] If therefore there be any of you that are of his people, let the Lord, even his Lord, be with him, and let him go up to Jerusalem that is in Judea, and build the house of the Lord of Israel: for he is the Lord that dwelleth in Jerusalem. [6] Whosoever then dwell in the places about, let them help him, those, I say, that are his neighbours, with gold, and with silver, [7] with gifts, with horses, and with cattle, and other things, which have been set forth by vow, for the temple of the Lord at Jerusalem. [8] Then the chief of the families of Judea and of the tribe of Benjamin stood up; the priests also, and the Levites, and all they whose mind the Lord had moved to go up, and to build an house for the Lord at Jerusalem, [9] and they that dwelt round about them, and helped them in all things with silver and gold, with horses and cattle, and with very many free gifts of a great number whose minds were stirred up thereto. [10] King Cyrus also brought forth the holy vessels, which Nabuchodonosor had carried away from Jerusalem, and had set up in his

temple of idols. [11] Now when Cyrus king of the Persians had brought them forth, he delivered them to Mithridates his treasurer: [12] and by him they were delivered to Sanabassar the governor of Judea. [13] And this was the number of them; A thousand golden cups, and a thousand of silver, censers of silver twenty nine, vials of gold thirty, and of silver two thousand four hundred and ten, and a thousand other vessels. [14] So all the vessels of gold and of silver, which were carried away, were five thousand four hundred threescore and nine. [15] These were brought back by Sanabassar, together with them of the captivity, from Babylon to Jerusalem. [16] But in the time of Artexerxes king of the Persians, Belemus, and Mithridates, and Tabellius, and Rathumus, and Beeltethmus, and Semellius the secretary, with others that were in commission with them, dwelling in Samaria and other places, wrote unto him against them that dwelt in Judea and Jerusalem these letters following; [17] To king Artexerxes our lord, Thy servants, Rathumus the storywriter, and Semellius the scribe, and the rest of their council, and the judges that are in Celosyria and Phenice. [18] Be it now known to the lord king, that the Jews that are come up from you to us, being come into Jerusalem, that rebellious and wicked city, do build the marketplaces, and repair the walls of it and do lay the foundation of the temple. [19] Now if this city and the walls thereof be made up again, they will not only refuse to give tribute, but also rebel against kings. [20] And forasmuch as the things pertaining to the temple are now in hand, we think it meet not to neglect such a matter, [21] but to speak unto our lord the king, to the intent that, if it be thy pleasure it may be sought out in the books of thy fathers: [22] And thou shalt find in the chronicles what is written concerning these things, and shalt understand that that city was rebellious, troubling both kings and cities: [23] and that the Jews were rebellious, and raised always wars therein; for the which cause even this city was made desolate. [24] Wherefore now we do declare unto thee, O lord the king, that if this city be built again, and the walls thereof set up anew, thou shalt from henceforth have no passage into Celosyria and Phenice. [25] Then the king wrote back again to Rathumus the storywriter, to Beeltethmus, to Semellius the scribe, and to the rest that were in commission, and dwellers in Samaria and Syria and Phenice, after this manner; [26] I have read the epistle which ye have sent unto me: therefore I commanded to make diligent search, and it hath been found that that city was from the beginning practising against kings; [27] and the men therein were given to rebellion and war: and that mighty kings and fierce were in Jerusalem, who reigned and exacted tributes in Celosyria and Phenice. [28] Now therefore I have commanded to hinder those men from building the city, and heed to be taken that there be no more done in it; [29] and that those wicked workers proceed no further to the annoyance of kings. [30] Then king Artexerxes his letters being read, Rathumus, and Semellius the scribe, and the rest that were in commission with them, removing in haste toward Jerusalem with a troop of horsemen and a multitude of people in battle array, began to hinder the builders; and the building of the temple in Jerusalem ceased until the second year of the reign of Darius king of the Persians.

3 [1] Now when Darius reigned, he made a great feast unto all his subjects, and unto all his household, and unto all the princes of Media and Persia, [2] and to all the gover-

nors and captains and lieutenants that were under him, from India unto Ethiopia, of an hundred twenty and seven provinces. [3] And when they had eaten and drunken, and being satisfied were gone home, then Darius the king went into his bedchamber, and slept, and soon after awaked. [4] Then three young men, that were of the guard that kept the king's body, spake one to another; [5] let every one of us speak a sentence: he that shall overcome, and whose sentence shall seem wiser than the others, unto him shall the king Darius give great gifts, and great things in token of victory: [6] as, to be clothed in purple, to drink in gold, and to sleep upon gold, and a chariot with bridles of gold, and an headtire of fine linen, and a chain about his neck: [7] And he shall sit next to Darius because of his wisdom, and shall be called Darius his cousin. [8] And then every one wrote his sentence, sealed it, and laid it under king Darius his pillow; [9] and said that, when the king is risen, some will give him the writings; and of whose side the king and the three princes of Persia shall judge that his sentence is the wisest, to him shall the victory be given, as was appointed. [10] The first wrote, Wine is the strongest. [11] The second wrote, The king is strongest. [12] The third wrote, Women are strongest: but above all things Truth beareth away the victory. [13] Now when the king was risen up, they took their writings, and delivered them unto him, and so he read them: [14] And sending forth he called all the princes of Persia and Media, and the governors, and the captains, and the lieutenants, and the chief officers; [15] and sat him down in the royal seat of judgment; and the writings were read before them. [16] And he said, Call the young men, and they shall declare their own sentences. So they were called, and came in. [17] And he said unto them, Declare unto us your mind concerning the writings. Then began the first, who had spoken of the strength of wine; [18] and he said thus, O ye men, how exceeding strong is wine! it causeth all men to err that drink it: [19] It maketh the mind of the king and of the fatherless child to be all one; of the bondman and of the freeman, of the poor man and of the rich: [20] It turneth also every thought into jollity and mirth, so that a man remembereth neither sorrow nor debt: [21] And it maketh every heart rich, so that a man remembereth neither king nor governor; and it maketh to speak all things by talents: [22] And when they are in their cups, they forget their love both to friends and brethren, and a little after draw out swords: [23] But when they are from the wine, they remember not what they have done. [24] O ye men, is not wine the strongest, that enforceth to do thus? And when he had so spoken, he held his peace.

4 [1] Then the second, that had spoken of the strength of the king, began to say, [2] O ye men, do not men excel in strength that bear rule over sea and land and all things in them? [3] But yet the king is more mighty: for he is lord of all these things, and hath dominion over them; and whatsoever he commandeth them they do. [4] If he bid them make war the one against the other, they do it: if he send them out against the enemies, they go, and break down mountains, walls, and towers. [5] They slay and are slain, and transgress not the king's commandment: if they get the victory, they bring all to the king, as well the spoil, as all things else. [6] Likewise for those that are no soldiers, and have not to do with wars, but use husbandry, when they have reaped again that which they had sown, they bring it to the king,

and compel one another to pay tribute unto the king. [7] And yet he is but one man: if he command to kill, they kill; if he command to spare, they spare; [8] if he command to smite, they smite; if he command to make desolate, they make desolate; if he command to build, they build; [9] if he command to cut down, they cut down; if he command to plant, they plant. [10] So all his people and his armies obey him: furthermore he lieth down, he eateth and drinketh, and taketh his rest: [11] and these keep watch round about him, neither may any one depart, and do his own business, neither disobey they him in any thing. [12] O ye men, how should not the king be mightiest, when in such sort he is obeyed? And he held his tongue. [13] Then the third, who had spoken of women, and of the truth, (this was Zorobabel) began to speak. [14] O ye men, it is not the great king, nor the multitude of men, neither is it wine that excelleth; who is it then that ruleth them, or hath the lordship over them? are they not women? [15] Women have borne the king and all the people that bear rule by sea and land. [16] Even of them came they: and they nourished them up that planted the vineyards, from whence the wine cometh. [17] These also make garments for men; these bring glory unto men; and without women cannot men be. [18] Yea, and if men have gathered together gold and silver, or any other goodly thing, do they not love a woman which is comely in favour and beauty? [19] And letting all those things go, do they not gape, and even with open mouth fix their eyes fast on her; and have not all men more desire unto her than unto silver or gold, or any goodly thing whatsoever? [20] A man leaveth his own father that brought him up, and his own country, and cleaveth unto his wife. [21] He sticketh not to spend his life with his wife and remembereth neither father, nor mother, nor country. [22] By this also ye must know that women have dominion over you: do ye not labour and toil, and give and bring all to the woman? [23] Yea, a man taketh his sword, and goeth his way to rob and to steal, to sail upon the sea and upon rivers; [24] and looketh upon a lion, and goeth in the darkness; and when he hath stolen, spoiled, and robbed, he bringeth it to his love. [25] Wherefore a man loveth his wife better than father or mother. [26] Yea, many there be that have run out of their wits for women, and become servants for their sakes. [27] Many also have perished, have erred, and sinned, for women. [28] And now do ye not believe me? is not the king great in his power? do not all regions fear to touch him? [29] Yet did I see him and Apame the king's concubine, the daughter of the admirable Bartacus, sitting at the right hand of the king, [30] and taking the crown from the king's head, and setting it upon her own head; she also struck the king with her left hand. [31] And yet for all this the king gaped and gazed upon her with open mouth: if she laughed upon him, he laughed also: but if she took any displeasure at him, the king was fain to flatter, that she might be reconciled to him again. [32] O ye men, how can it be but women should be strong, seeing they do thus? [33] Then the king and the princes looked one upon another: so he began to speak of the truth. [34] O ye men, are not women strong? great is the earth, high is the heaven, swift is the sun in his course, for he compasseth the heavens round about, and fetcheth his course again to his own place in one day. [35] Is he not great that maketh these things? therefore great is the truth, and stronger than all things. [36] All the earth calleth upon the truth, and the heaven blesseth it: all works shake and tremble at it, and with it is no unrighteous thing. [37] Wine is wicked, the king is wicked, women are wicked, all the children of men are wicked, and such are all their wicked works; and there is no truth in them; in their unrighteousness also they shall perish. [38] As for the truth, it endureth, and is always strong; it liveth and conquereth for evermore. [39] With her there is no accepting of persons or rewards; but she doeth the things that are just, and refraineth from all unjust and wicked things; and all men do well like of her works. [40] Neither in her judgment is any unrighteousness; and she is the strength, kingdom, power, and majesty of all ages. Blessed be the God of truth. [41] And with that he held his peace. And all the people then shouted, and said, Great is Truth, and mighty above all things. [42] Then said the king unto him, Ask what thou wilt more than is appointed in the writing, and we will give it thee, because thou art found wisest; and thou shalt sit next me, and shalt be called my cousin. [43] Then said he unto the king, Remember thy vow, which thou hast vowed to build Jerusalem, in the day when thou camest to thy kingdom, [44] and to send away all the vessels that were taken away out of Jerusalem, which Cyrus set apart, when he vowed to destroy Babylon, and to send them again thither. [45] Thou also hast vowed to build up the temple, which the Edomites burned when Judea was made desolate by the Chaldees. [46] And now, O lord the king, this is that which I require, and which I desire of thee, and this is the princely liberality proceeding from thyself: I desire therefore that thou make good the vow, the performance whereof with thine own mouth thou hast vowed to the King of heaven. [47] Then Darius the king stood up, and kissed him, and wrote letters for him unto all the treasurers and lieutenants and captains and governors, that they should safely convey on their way both him, and all those that go up with him to build Jerusalem. [48] He wrote letters also unto the lieutenants that were in Celosyria and Phenice, and unto them in Libanus, that they should bring cedar wood from Libanus unto Jerusalem, and that they should build the city with him. [49] Moreover he wrote for all the Jews that went out of his realm up into Jewry, concerning their freedom, that no officer, no ruler, no lieutenant, nor treasurer, should forcibly enter into their doors; [50] and that all the country which they hold should be free without tribute; and that the Edomites should give over the villages of the Jews which then they held: [51] Yea, that there should be yearly given twenty talents to the building of the temple, until the time that it were built; [52] and other ten talents yearly, to maintain the burnt offerings upon the altar every day, as they had a commandment to offer seventeen: [53] and that all they that went from Babylon to build the city should have free liberty, as well they as their posterity, and all the priests that went away. [54] He wrote also concerning the charges, and the priests' vestments wherein they minister; [55] and likewise for the charges of the Levites, to be given them until the day that the house were finished, and Jerusalem builded up. [56] And he commanded to give to all that kept the city pensions and wages. [57] He sent away also all the vessels from Babylon, that Cyrus had set apart; and all that Cyrus had given in commandment, the same charged he also to be done, and sent unto Jerusalem. [58] Now when this young man was gone forth, he lifted up his face to heaven toward Jerusalem, and praised the King of heaven, [59] and said, From thee cometh victory, from thee cometh wisdom, and thine is the glory, and I am thy servant. [60] Blessed art thou, who hast given me wisdom: for to thee I give thanks, O Lord of our fathers. [61] And so he took the letters, and went out, and came unto Babylon, and told it all his brethren. [62] And they praised the God of their fathers, because he had given them freedom and liberty [63] to go up, and to build Jerusalem, and the temple which is called by his name: and they feasted with instruments of music and gladness seven days.

5 [1] After this were the principal men of the families chosen according to their tribes, to go up with their wives and sons and daughters, with their menservants and maidservants, and their cattle. [2] And Darius sent with them a thousand horsemen, till they had brought them back to Jerusalem safely, and with musical [instruments] tabrets and flutes. [3] And all their brethren played, and he made them go up together with them. [4] And these are the names of the men which went up, according to their families among their tribes, after their several heads. [5] The priests, the sons of Phinees the son of Aaron: Jesus the son of Josedec, the son of Saraias, and Joacim the son of Zorobabel, the son of Salathiel, of the house of David, out of the kindred of Phares, of the tribe of Judah; [6] who spake wise sentences before Darius the king of Persia in the second year of his reign, in the month Nisan, which is the first month. [7] And these are they of Jewry that came up from the captivity, where they dwelt as strangers, whom Nabuchodonosor the king of Babylon had carried away unto Babylon. [8] And they returned unto Jerusalem, and to the other parts of Jewry, every man to his own city, who came with Zorobabel, with Jesus, Nehemias, and Zacharias, and Reesaias, Enenius, Mardocheus,

Beelsarus, Aspharasus, Reelius, Roimus, and Baana, their guides. [9] The number of them of the nation, and their governors, sons of Phoros, two thousand an hundred seventy and two; the sons of Saphat, four hundred seventy and two: [10] the sons of Ares, seven hundred fifty and six: [11] the sons of Phaath Moab, two thousand eight hundred and twelve: [12] the sons of Elam, a thousand two hundred fifty and four: the sons of Zathul, nine hundred forty and five: the sons of Corbe, seven hundred and five: the sons of Bani, six hundred forty and eight: [13] the sons of Bebai, six hundred twenty and three: the sons of Sadas, three thousand two hundred twenty and two: [14] the sons of Adonikam, six hundred sixty and seven: the sons of Bagoi, two thousand sixty and six: the sons of Adin, four hundred fifty and four: [15] the sons of Aterezias, ninety and two: the sons of Ceilan and Azetas, threescore and seven: the sons of Azuran, four hundred thirty and two: [16] the sons of Ananias, an hundred and one: the sons of Arom, thirty two: and the sons of Bassa, three hundred twenty and three: the sons of Azephurith, an hundred and two: [17] the sons of Meterus, three thousand and five: the sons of Bethlomon, an hundred twenty and three: [18] they of Netophah, fifty and five: they of Anathoth, an hundred fifty and eight: they of Bethsamos, forty and two: [19] they of Kiriathiarius, twenty and five: they of Caphira and Beroth, seven hundred forty and three: they of Pira, seven hundred: [20] they of Chadias and Ammidoi, four hundred twenty and two: they of Cirama and Gabdes, six hundred twenty and one: [21] they of Macalon, an hundred twenty and two: they of Betolius, fifty and two: the sons of Nephis, an hundred fifty and six: [22] the sons of Calamolalus and Onus, seven hundred twenty and five: the sons of Jerechus, two hundred forty and five: [23] the sons of Annas, three thousand three hundred and thirty. [24] The priests: the sons of Jeddu, the son of Jesus, among the sons of Sanasib, nine hundred seventy and two: the sons of Meruth, a thousand fifty and two: [25] the sons of Phassaron, a thousand forty and seven: the sons of Carme, a thousand and seventeen. [26] The Levites: the sons of Jessue, and Cadmiel, and Banuas, and Sudias, seventy and four. [27] The holy singers: the sons of Asaph, an hundred twenty and eight. [28] The porters: the sons of Salum, the sons of Jatal, the sons of Talmon, the sons of Dacobi, the sons of Teta, the sons of Sami, in all an hundred thirty and nine. [29] The servants of the temple: the sons of Esau, the sons of Asipha, the sons of Tabaoth, the sons of Ceras, the sons of Sud, the sons of Phaleas, the sons of Labana, the sons of Graba, [30] the sons of Acua, the sons of Uta, the sons of Cetab, the sons of Agaba, the sons of Subai, the sons of Anan, the sons of Cathua, the sons of Geddur, [31] the sons of Airus, the sons of Daisan, the sons of Noeba, the sons of Chaseba, the sons of Gazera, the sons of Azia, the sons of Phinees, the sons of Azare, the sons of Bastai, the sons of Asana, the sons of Meani, the sons of Naphisi, the sons of Acub, the sons of Acipha, the sons of Assur, the sons of Pharacim, the sons of Basaloth, [32] the sons of Meeda, the sons of Coutha, the sons of Charea, the sons of Charcus, the sons of Aserer, the sons of Thomoi, the sons of Nasith, the sons of Atipha. [33] The sons of the servants of Solomon: the sons of Azaphion, the sons of Pharira, the sons of Jeeli, the sons of Lozon, the sons of Israel, the sons of Sapheth, [34] the sons of Hagia, the sons of Pharacareth, the sons of Sabi, the sons of Sarothie, the sons of Masias, the sons of Gar, the sons of Addus, the sons of Suba, the sons of

Apherra, the sons of Barodis, the sons of Sabat, the sons of Allom. [35] All the ministers of the temple, and the sons of the servants of Solomon, were three hundred seventy and two. [36] These came up from Thermeleth and Thelersas, Charaathalar leading them, and Aalar; [37] neither could they shew their families, nor their stock, how they were of Israel: the sons of Ladan, the sons of Ban, the sons of Necodan, six hundred fifty and two. [38] And of the priests that usurped the office of the priesthood, and were not found: the sons of Obdia, the sons of Accoz, the sons of Addus, who married Augia one of the daughters of Barzelus, and was named after his name. [39] And when the description of the kindred of these men was sought in the register, and was not found, they were removed from executing the office of the priesthood: [40] For unto them said Nehemias and Atharias, that they should not be partakers of the holy things, till there arose up an high priest clothed with doctrine and truth. [41] So of Israel, from them of twelve years old and upward, they were all in number forty thousand, besides menservants and womenservants, two thousand three hundred and sixty. [42] Their menservants and handmaids were seven thousand three hundred forty and seven: the singing men and singing women, two hundred forty and five: [43] four hundred thirty and five camels, seven thousand thirty and six horses, two hundred forty and five mules, five thousand five hundred twenty and five beasts used to the yoke. [44] And certain of the chief of their families, when they came to the temple of God that is in Jerusalem, vowed to set up the house again in his own place according to their ability, [45] and to give into the holy treasury of the works a thousand pounds of gold, five thousand of silver, and an hundred priestly vestments. [46] And so dwelt the priests and the Levites and the people in Jerusalem, and in the country, the singers also and the porters; and all Israel in their villages. [47] But when the seventh month was at hand, and when the children of Israel were every man in his own place, they came all together with one consent into the open place of the first gate which is toward the east. [48] Then stood up Jesus the son of Josedec, and his brethren the priests and Zorobabel the son of Salathiel, and his brethren, and made ready the altar of the God of Israel, [49] to offer burnt sacrifices upon it, according as it is expressly commanded in the book of Moses the man of God. [50] And there were gathered unto them out of the other nations of the land, and they erected the altar upon his own place, because all the nations of the land were at enmity with them, and oppressed them; and they offered sacrifices according to the time, and burnt offerings to the Lord both morning and evening. [51] Also they held the feast of tabernacles, as it is commanded in the law, and offered sacrifices daily, as was meet: [52] And after that, the continual oblations, and the sacrifice of the sabbaths, and of the new moons, and of all holy feasts. [53] And all they that had made any vow to God began to offer sacrifices to God from the first day of the seventh month, although the temple of the Lord was not yet built. [54] And they gave unto the masons and carpenters money, meat, and drink, with cheerfulness. [55] Unto them of Zidon also and Tyre they gave carts, that they should bring cedar trees from Libanus, which should be brought by floats to the haven of Joppa, according as it was commanded them by Cyrus king of the Persians. [56] And in the second year and second month after his coming to the temple of God at Jerusalem began Zorobabel the son of Salathiel, and Jesus the son of Josedec, and their brethren, and the priests, and the Levites, and all they that were come unto Jerusalem out of the captivity: [57] And they laid the foundation of the house of God in the first day of the second month, in the second year after they were come to Jewry and Jerusalem. [58] And they appointed the Levites from twenty years old over the works of the Lord. Then stood up Jesus, and his sons and brethren, and Cadmiel his brother, and the sons of Madiabun, with the sons of Joda the son of Eliadun, with their sons and brethren, all Levites, with one accord setters forward of the business, labouring to advance the works in the house of God. So the workmen built the temple of the Lord. [59] And the priests stood arrayed in their vestments with musical instruments and trumpets; and the Levites the sons of Asaph had cymbals, [60] singing songs of thanksgiving, and praising the Lord, according as David the king of Israel had ordained. [61] And they sung with loud voices songs to the praise of the Lord, because his mercy and glory is for ever in all Israel. [62] And all the people sounded trumpets, and shouted with a loud voice, singing songs of thanksgiving unto the Lord for the rearing up of the house of the Lord. [63] Also of the priests and Levites, and of the chief of their families, the ancients who had seen the former house came to the building of this with weeping and great crying. [64] But many with trumpets and joy shouted with loud voice, [65] insomuch that the trumpets might not be heard for the weeping of the people: yet the multitude sounded marvellously, so that it was heard afar off. [66] Wherefore when the enemies of the tribe of Judah and Benjamin heard it, they came to know what that noise of trumpets should mean. [67] And they perceived that they that were of the captivity did build the temple unto the Lord God of Israel. [68] So they went to Zorobabel and Jesus, and to the chief of the families, and said unto them, We will build together with you. [69] For we likewise, as ye, do obey your Lord, and do sacrifice unto him from the days of Azbazareth the king of the Assyrians, who brought us hither. [70] Then Zorobabel and Jesus and the chief of the families of Israel said unto them, It is not for us and you to build together an house unto the Lord our God. [71] We ourselves alone will build unto the Lord of Israel, according as Cyrus the king of the Persians hath commanded us. [72] But the heathen of the land lying heavy upon the inhabitants of Judea, and holding them strait, hindered their building; [73] and by their secret plots, and popular persuasions and commotions, they hindered the finishing of the building all the time that king Cyrus lived: so they were hindered from building for the space of two years, until the reign of Darius.

6 [1] Now in the second year of the reign of Darius, Aggeus and Zacharias the son of Addo, the prophets, prophesied unto the Jews in Jewry and Jerusalem in the name of the Lord God of Israel, which was upon them. [2] Then stood up Zorobabel the son of Salathiel, and Jesus the son of Josedec, and began to build the house of the Lord at Jerusalem, the prophets of the Lord being with them, and helping them. [3] At the same time came unto them Sisinnes the governor of Syria and Phenice, with Sathrabuzanes and his companions, and said unto them, [4] By whose appointment do ye build this house and this roof, and perform all the other things? and who are the workmen that perform these things? [5] Nevertheless the elders of the Jews obtained favour, because the Lord had visited the captivity; [6] and they

were not hindered from building, until such time as signification was given unto Darius concerning them, and an answer received. [7] The copy of the letters which Sisinnes, governor of Syria and Phenice, and Sathrabuzanes, with their companions, rulers in Syria and Phenice, wrote and sent unto Darius; To king Darius, greeting: [8] Let all things be known unto our lord the king, that being come into the country of Judea, and entered into the city of Jerusalem we found in the city of Jerusalem the ancients of the Jews that were of the captivity [9] building an house unto the Lord, great and new, of hewn and costly stones, and the timber already laid upon the walls. [10] And those works are done with great speed, and the work goeth on prosperously in their hands, and with all glory and diligence is it made. [11] Then asked we these elders, saying, By whose commandment build ye this house, and lay the foundations of these works? [12] Therefore to the intent that we might give knowledge unto thee by writing, we demanded of them who were the chief doers, and we required of them the names in writing of their principal men. [13] So they gave us this answer, We are the servants of the Lord which made heaven and earth. [14] And as for this house, it was builded many years ago by a king of Israel great and strong, and was finished. [15] But when our fathers provoked God unto wrath, and sinned against the Lord of Israel which is in heaven, he gave them over into the power of Nabuchodonosor king of Babylon, of the Chaldees; [16] who pulled down the house, and burned it, and carried away the people captives unto Babylon. [17] But in the first year that king Cyrus reigned over the country of Babylon, Cyrus the king wrote to build up this house. [18] And the holy vessels of gold and of silver that Nabuchodonosor had carried away out of the house at Jerusalem, and had set them in his own temple, those Cyrus the king brought forth again out of the temple at Babylon, and they were delivered to Zorobabel and to Sanabassarus the ruler, [19] with commandment that he should carry away the same vessels, and put them in the temple at Jerusalem; and that the temple of the Lord should be built in his place. [20] Then the same Sanabassarus, being come hither, laid the foundations of the house of the Lord at Jerusalem; and from that time to this being still a building, it is not yet fully ended. [21] Now therefore, if it seem good unto the king, let search be made among the records of king Cyrus: [22] And if it be found that the building of the house of the Lord at Jerusalem hath been done with the consent of king Cyrus, and if our lord the king be so minded, let him signify unto us thereof. [23] Then commanded king Darius to seek among the records at Babylon: and so at Ecbatane the palace, which is in the country of Media, there was found a roll wherein these things were recorded. [24] In the first year of the reign of Cyrus, king Cyrus commanded that the house of the Lord at Jerusalem should be built again, where they do sacrifice with continual fire: [25] whose height shall be sixty cubits and the breadth sixty cubits, with three rows of hewn stones, and one row of new wood of that country; and the expenses thereof to be given out of the house of king Cyrus: [26] and that the holy vessels of the house of the Lord, both of gold and silver, that Nabuchodonosor took out of the house at Jerusalem, and brought to Babylon, should be restored to the house at Jerusalem, and be set in the place where they were before. [27] And also he commanded that Sisinnes the governor of Syria and Phenice, and Sathrabuzanes, and their companions, and those which were appointed rulers in Syria and Phenice, should be careful not to meddle with the place, but suffer Zorobabel, the servant of the Lord, and governor of Judea, and the elders of the Jews, to build the house of the Lord in that place. [28] I have commanded also to have it built up whole again; and that they look diligently to help those that be of the captivity of the Jews, till the house of the Lord be finished: [29] And out of the tribute of Celosyria and Phenice a portion carefully to be given these men for the sacrifices of the Lord, that is, to Zorobabel the governor, for bullocks, and rams, and lambs; [30] and also corn, salt, wine, and oil, and that continually every year without further question, according as the priests that be in Jerusalem shall signify to be daily spent: [31] that offerings may be made to the most high God for the king and for his children, and that they may pray for their lives. [32] And he commanded that whosoever should transgress, yea, or make light of any thing afore spoken or written, out of his own house should a tree be taken, and he thereon be hanged, and all his goods seized for the king. [33] The Lord therefore, whose name is there called upon, utterly destroy every king and nation, that stretcheth out his hand to hinder or endamage that house of the Lord in Jerusalem. [34] I Darius the king have ordained that according unto these things it be done with diligence.

7 [1] Then Sisinnes the governor of Celosyria and Phenice, and Sathrabuzanes, with their companions following the commandments of king Darius, [2] did very carefully oversee the holy works, assisting the ancients of the Jews and governors of the temple. [3] And so the holy works prospered, when Aggeus and Zacharias the prophets prophesied. [4] And they finished these things

by the commandment of the Lord God of Israel, and with the consent of Cyrus, Darius, and Artexerxes, kings of Persia. [5] And thus was the holy house finished in the three and twentieth day of the month Adar, in the sixth year of Darius king of the Persians. [6] And the children of Israel, the priests, and the Levites, and others that were of the captivity, that were added unto them, did according to the things written in the book of Moses. [7] And to the dedication of the temple of the Lord they offered an hundred bullocks, two hundred rams, four hundred lambs; [8] and twelve goats for the sin of all Israel, according to the number of the chief of the tribes of Israel. [9] The priests also and the Levites stood arrayed in their vestments, according to their kindreds, in the service of the Lord God of Israel, according to the book of Moses: and the porters at every gate. [10] And the children of Israel that were of the captivity held the passover the fourteenth day of the first month, after that the priests and the Levites were sanctified. [11] They that were of the captivity were not all sanctified together: but the Levites were all sanctified together. [12] And so they offered the passover for all them of the captivity, and for their brethren the priests, and for themselves. [13] And the children of Israel that came out of the captivity did eat, even all they that had separated themselves from the abominations of the people of the land, and sought the Lord. [14] And they kept the feast of unleavened bread seven days, making merry before the Lord, [15] for that he had turned the counsel of the king of Assyria toward them, to strengthen their hands in the works of the Lord God of Israel.

8 [1] And after these things, when Artexerxes the king of the Persians reigned, came Esdras the son of Saraias,

the son of Ezerias, the son of Helchiah, the son of Salum, [2] the son of Sadduc, the son of Achitob, the son of Amarias, the son of Ezias, the son of Meremoth, the son of Zaraias, the son of Savias, the son of Boccas, the son of Abisum, the son of Phinees, the son of Eleazar, the son of Aaron the chief priest. [3] This Esdras went up from Babylon, as a scribe, being very ready in the law of Moses, that was given by the God of Israel. [4] And the king did him honour: for he found grace in his sight in all his requests. [5] There went up with him also certain of the children of Israel, of the priests of the Levites, of the holy singers, porters, and ministers of the temple, unto Jerusalem. [6] In the seventh year of the reign of Artexerxes, in the fifth month, this was the king's seventh year; for they went from Babylon in the first day of the first month, and came to Jerusalem, according to the prosperous journey which the Lord gave them. [7] For Esdras had very great skill, so that he omitted nothing of the law and commandments of the Lord, but taught all Israel the ordinances and judgments. [8] Now the copy of the commission, which was written from Artexerxes the king, and came to Esdras the priest and reader of the law of the Lord, is this that followeth: [9] King Artexerxes unto Esdras the priest and reader of the law of the Lord sendeth greeting: [10] Having determined to deal graciously, I have given order, that such of the nation of the Jews, and of the priests and Levites being within our realm, as are willing and desirous, should go with thee unto Jerusalem. [11] As many therefore as have a mind thereunto, let them depart with thee, as it hath seemed good both to me and my seven friends the counsellors; [12] that they may look unto the affairs of Judea and Jerusalem, agreeably to that which is in the law of the Lord; [13] and carry the gifts unto the

Lord of Israel to Jerusalem, which I and my friends have vowed, and all the gold and silver that in the country of Babylon can be found, to the Lord in Jerusalem, [14] with that also which is given of the people for the temple of the Lord their God at Jerusalem: and that silver and gold may be collected for bullocks, rams, and lambs, and things thereunto appertaining; [15] to the end that they may offer sacrifices unto the Lord upon the altar of the Lord their God, which is in Jerusalem. [16] And whatsoever thou and thy brethren will do with the silver and gold, that do, according to the will of thy God. [17] And the holy vessels of the Lord, which are given thee for the use of the temple of thy God, which is in Jerusalem, thou shalt set before thy God in Jerusalem. [18] And whatsoever thing else thou shalt remember for the use of the temple of thy God, thou shalt give it out of the king's treasury. [19] And I king Artexerxes have also commanded the keepers of the treasures in Syria and Phenice, that whatsoever Esdras the priest and the reader of the law of the most high God shall send for, they should give it him with speed, [20] to the sum of an hundred talents of silver, likewise also of wheat even to an hundred cors, and an hundred pieces of wine, and other things in abundance. [21] Let all things be performed after the law of God diligently unto the most high God, that wrath come not upon the kingdom of the king and his sons. [22] I command you also, that ye require no tax, nor any other imposition, of any of the priests, or Levites, or holy singers, or porters, or ministers of the temple, or of any that have doings in this temple, and that no man have authority to impose any thing upon them. [23] And thou, Esdras, according to the wisdom of God, ordain judges and justices, that they may judge in all Syria and Phenice all those that know the law of thy God; and those that know it not thou shalt teach. [24] And whosoever shall transgress the law of thy God, and of the king, shall be punished diligently, whether it be by death, or other punishment, by penalty of money, or by imprisonment. [25] Then said Esdras the scribe, Blessed be the only Lord God of my fathers, who hath put these things into the heart of the king, to glorify his house that is in Jerusalem: [26] and hath honoured me in the sight of the king, and his counsellors, and all his friends and nobles. [27] Therefore was I encouraged by the help of the Lord my God, and gathered together men of Israel to go up with me. [28] And these are the chief according to their families and several dignities, that went up with me from Babylon in the reign of king Artexerxes: [29] of the sons of Phinees, Gerson: of the sons of Ithamar, Gamael: of the sons of David, Lettus the son of Sechenias: [30] of the sons of Pharez, Zacharias; and with him were counted an hundred and fifty men: [31] of the sons of Pahath Moab, Eliaonias, the son of Zaraias, and with him two hundred men: [32] of the sons of Zathoe, Sechenias the son of Jezelus, and with him three hundred men: of the sons of Adin, Obeth the son of Jonathan, and with him two hundred and fifty men: [33] of the sons of Elam, Josias son of Gotholias, and with him seventy men: [34] of the sons of Saphatias, Zaraias son of Michael, and with him threescore and ten men: [35] of the sons of Joab, Abadias son of Jezelus, and with him two hundred and twelve men: [36] of the sons of Banid, Assalimoth son of Josaphias, and with him an hundred and threescore men: [37] of the sons of Babi, Zacharias son of Bebai, and with him twenty and eight men: [38] of the sons of Astath, Johannes son of Acatan, and with him an hundred and ten men: [39] of the sons of Adonikam the last, and these are the names of them, Eliphalet, Jewel, and Samaias, and with them seventy men: [40] of the sons of Bago, Uthi the son of Istalcurus, and with him seventy men. [41] And these I gathered together to the river called Theras, where we pitched our tents three days: and then I surveyed them. [42] But when I had found there none of the priests and Levites, [43] then sent I unto Eleazar, and Iduel, and Masman, [44] and Alnathan, and Mamaias, and Joribas, and Nathan, Eunatan, Zacharias, and Mosollamon, principal men and learned. [45] And I bade them that they should go unto Saddeus the captain, who was in the place of the treasury: [46] and commanded them that they should speak unto Daddeus, and to his brethren, and to the treasurers in that place, to send us such men as might execute the priests' office in the house of the Lord. [47] And by the mighty hand of our Lord they brought unto us skilful men of the sons of Moli the son of Levi, the son of Israel, Asebebia, and his sons, and his brethren, who were eighteen. [48] And Asebia, and Annus, and Osaias his brother, of the sons of Channuneus, and their sons, were twenty men. [49] And of the servants of the temple whom David had ordained, and the principal men for the service of the Levites to wit, the servants of the temple two hundred and twenty, the catalogue of whose names were shewed. [50] And there I vowed a fast unto the young men before our Lord, to desire of him a prosperous journey both for us and them that were with us, for our children, and for the cattle: [51] for I was ashamed to ask the king footmen, and horsemen, and conduct for safeguard against our adversaries. [52] For we had said unto the king, that the power of the Lord our God should be with them that seek him, to support them in all ways.

[53] And again we besought our Lord as touching these things, and found him favourable unto us. [54] Then I separated twelve of the chief of the priests, Esebrias, and Assanias, and ten men of their brethren with them: [55] and I weighed them the gold, and the silver, and the holy vessels of the house of our Lord, which the king, and his council, and the princes, and all Israel, had given. [56] And when I had weighed it, I delivered unto them six hundred and fifty talents of silver, and silver vessels of an hundred talents, and an hundred talents of gold, [57] and twenty golden vessels, and twelve vessels of brass, even of fine brass, glittering like gold. [58] And I said unto them, Both ye are holy unto the Lord, and the vessels are holy, and the gold and the silver is a vow unto the Lord, the Lord of our fathers. [59] Watch ye, and keep them till ye deliver them to the chief of the priests and Levites, and to the principal men of the families of Israel, in Jerusalem, into the chambers of the house of our God. [60] So the priests and the Levites, who had received the silver and the gold and the vessels, brought them unto Jerusalem, into the temple of the Lord. [61] And from the river Theras we departed the twelfth day of the first month, and came to Jerusalem by the mighty hand of our Lord, which was with us: and from the beginning of our journey the Lord delivered us from every enemy, and so we came to Jerusalem. [62] And when we had been there three days, the gold and silver that was weighed was delivered in the house of our Lord on the fourth day unto Marmoth the priest the son of Iri. [63] And with him was Eleazar the son of Phinees, and with them were Josabad the son of Jesu and Moeth the son of Sabban, Levites: all was delivered them by number and weight. [64] And all the weight of them was written up the same hour.

[65] Moreover they that were come out of the captivity offered sacrifice unto the Lord God of Israel, even twelve bullocks for all Israel, fourscore and sixteen rams, [66] threescore and twelve lambs, goats for a peace offering, twelve; all of them a sacrifice to the Lord. [67] And they delivered the king's commandments unto the king's stewards, and to the governors of Celosyria and Phenice; and they honoured the people and the temple of God. [68] Now when these things were done, the rulers came unto me, and said, [69] The nation of Israel, the princes, the priests, and Levites, have not put away from them the strange people of the land, nor the pollutions of the Gentiles to wit, of the Canaanites, Hittites, Pheresites, Jebusites, and the Moabites, Egyptians, and Edomites. [70] For both they and their sons have married with their daughters, and the holy seed is mixed with the strange people of the land; and from the beginning of this matter the rulers and the great men have been partakers of this iniquity. [71] And as soon as I had heard these things, I rent my clothes, and the holy garment, and pulled off the hair from off my head and beard, and sat me down sad and very heavy. [72] So all they that were then moved at the word of the Lord God of Israel assembled unto me, whilst I mourned for the iniquity: but I sat still full of heaviness until the evening sacrifice. [73] Then rising up from the fast with my clothes and the holy garment rent, and bowing my knees, and stretching forth my hands unto the Lord, [74] I said, O Lord, I am confounded and ashamed before thy face; [75] for our sins are multiplied above our heads, and our ignorances have reached up unto heaven. [76] For ever since the time of our fathers we have been and are in great sin, even unto this day. [77] And for our sins and our fathers' we with our

brethren and our kings and our priests were given up unto the kings of the earth, to the sword, and to captivity, and for a prey with shame, unto this day. [78] And now in some measure hath mercy been shewed unto us from thee, O Lord, that there should be left us a root and a name in the place of thy sanctuary; [79] and to discover unto us a light in the house of the Lord our God, and to give us food in the time of our servitude. [80] Yea, when we were in bondage, we were not forsaken of our Lord; but he made us gracious before the kings of Persia, so that they gave us food; [81] yea, and honoured the temple of our Lord, and raised up the desolate Sion, that they have given us a sure abiding in Jewry and Jerusalem. [82] And now, O Lord, what shall we say, having these things? for we have transgressed thy commandments, which thou gavest by the hand of thy servants the prophets, saying, [83] that the land, which ye enter into to possess as an heritage, is a land polluted with the pollutions of the strangers of the land, and they have filled it with their uncleanness. [84] Therefore now shall ye not join your daughters unto their sons, neither shall ye take their daughters unto your sons. [85] Moreover ye shall never seek to have peace with them, that ye may be strong, and eat the good things of the land, and that ye may leave the inheritance of the land unto your children for evermore. [86] And all that is befallen is done unto us for our wicked works and great sins; for thou, O Lord, didst make our sins light, [87] and didst give unto us such a root: but we have turned back again to transgress thy law, and to mingle ourselves with the uncleanness of the nations of the land. [88] Mightest not thou be angry with us to destroy us, till thou hadst left us neither root, seed, nor name? [89] O Lord of Israel, thou art true: for we are left a root this day. [90] Behold, now are we before thee in our iniquities, for we cannot stand any longer by reason of these things before thee. [91] And as Esdras in his prayer made his confession, weeping, and lying flat upon the ground before the temple, there gathered unto him from Jerusalem a very great multitude of men and women and children: for there was great weeping among the multitude. [92] Then Jechonias the son of Jeelus, one of the sons of Israel, called out, and said, O Esdras, we have sinned against the Lord God, we have married strange women of the nations of the land, and now is all Israel aloft. [93] Let us make an oath to the Lord, that we will put away all our wives, which we have taken of the heathen, with their children, [94] like as thou hast decreed, and as many as do obey the law of the Lord. [95] Arise and put in execution: for to thee doth this matter appertain, and we will be with thee: do valiantly. [96] So Esdras arose, and took an oath of the chief of the priests and Levites of all Israel to do after these things; and so they sware.

9 [1] Then Esdras rising from the court of the temple went to the chamber of Joanan the son of Eliasib, [2] and remained there, and did eat no meat nor drink water, mourning for the great iniquities of the multitude. [3] And there was a proclamation in all Jewry and Jerusalem to all them that were of the captivity, that they should be gathered together at Jerusalem: [4] and that whosoever met not there within two or three days according as the elders that bare rule appointed, their cattle should be seized to the use of the temple, and himself cast out from them that were of the captivity. [5] And in three days were all they of the tribe of Judah and Benjamin gathered together at Jerusalem the twen-

tieth day of the ninth month. [6] And all the multitude sat trembling in the broad court of the temple because of the present foul weather. [7] So Esdras arose up, and said unto them, Ye have transgressed the law in marrying strange wives, thereby to increase the sins of Israel. [8] And now by confessing give glory unto the Lord God of our fathers, [9] and do his will, and separate yourselves from the heathen of the land, and from the strange women. [10] Then cried the whole multitude, and said with a loud voice, Like as thou hast spoken, so will we do. [11] But forasmuch as the people are many, and it is foul weather, so that we cannot stand without, and this is not a work of a day or two, seeing our sin in these things is spread far: [12] therefore let the rulers of the multitude stay, and let all them of our habitations that have strange wives come at the time appointed, [13] and with them the rulers and judges of every place, till we turn away the wrath of the Lord from us for this matter. [14] Then Jonathan the son of Azael and Ezechias the son of Theocanus accordingly took this matter upon them: and Mosollam and Levis and Sabbatheus helped them. [15] And they that were of the captivity did according to all these things. [16] And Esdras the priest chose unto him the principal men of their families, all by name: and in the first day of the tenth month they sat together to examine the matter. [17] So their cause that held strange wives was brought to an end in the first day of the first month. [18] And of the priests that were come together, and had strange wives, there were found: [19] of the sons of Jesus the son of Josedec, and his brethren; Matthelas and Eleazar, and Joribus and Joadanus. [20] And they gave their hands to put away their wives and to offer rams to make reconcilement for their errors. [21] And of the sons of Emmer; Ananias, and

Zabdeus, and Eanes, and Sameius, and Hiereel, and Azarias. [22] And of the sons of Phaisur; Elionas, Massias, Ismael, and Nathanael, and Ocidelus and Talsas. [23] And of the Levites; Jozabad, and Semis, and Colius, who was called Calitas, and Patheus, and Judas, and Jonas. [24] Of the holy singers; Eleazurus, Bacchurus. [25] Of the porters; Sallumus, and Tolbanes. [26] Of them of Israel, of the sons of Phoros; Hiermas, and Eddias, and Melchias, and Maelus, and Eleazar, and Asibias, and Baanias. [27] Of the sons of Ela; Matthanias, Zacharias, and Hierielus, and Hieremoth, and Aedias. [28] And of the sons of Zamoth; Eliadas, Elisimus, Othonias, Jarimoth, and Sabatus, and Sardeus. [29] Of the sons of Babai; Johannes, and Ananias, and Josabad, and Amatheis. [30] Of the sons of Mani; Olamus, Mamuchus, Jedeus, Jasubus, Jasael, and Hieremoth. [31] And of the sons of Addi; Naathus, and Moosias, Lacunus, and Naidus, and Mathanias, and Sesthel, Balnuus, and Manasseas. [32] And of the sons of Annas; Elionas, and Aseas, and Melchias, and Sabbeus, and Simon Chosameus. [33] And of the sons of Asom; Altaneus, and Matthias, and Baanaia, Eliphalet, and Manasses, and Semei. [34] And of the sons of Maani; Jeremias, Momdis, Omaerus, Juel, Mabdai, and Pelias, and Anos, Carabasion, and Enasibus, and Mamnitanaimus, Eliasis, Bannus, Eliali, Samis, Selemias, Nathanias: and of the sons of Ozora; Sesis, Esril, Azaelus, Samatus, Zambis, Josephus. [35] And of the sons of Ethma; Mazitias, Zabadaias, Edes, Juel, Banaias. [36] All these had taken strange wives, and they put them away with their children. [37] And the priests and Levites, and they that were of Israel, dwelt in Jerusalem, and in the country, in the first day of the seventh month: so the children of Israel were in their habitations. [38] And the whole multitude came together with one accord into the broad place of the holy porch toward the east: [39] and they spake unto Esdras the priest and reader, that he would bring the law of Moses, that was given of the Lord God of Israel. [40] So Esdras the chief priest brought the law unto the whole multitude from man to woman, and to all the priests, to hear the law in the first day of the seventh month. [41] And he read in the broad court before the holy porch from morning unto midday, before both men and women; and the multitude gave heed unto the law. [42] And Esdras the priest and reader of the law stood up upon a pulpit of wood, which was made for that purpose. [43] And there stood up by him Mattathias, Sammus, Ananias, Azarias, Urias, Ezecias, Balasamus, upon the right hand: [44] and upon his left hand stood Phaldaius, Misael, Melchias, Lothasubus, and Nabarias. [45] Then took Esdras the book of the law before the multitude: for he sat honourably in the first place in the sight of them all. [46] And when he opened the law, they stood all straight up. So Esdras blessed the Lord God most High, the God of hosts, Almighty. [47] And all the people answered, Amen; and lifting up their hands they fell to the ground, and worshipped the Lord. [48] Also Jesus, Anus, Sarabias, Adinus, Jacubus, Sabateas, Auteas, Maianeas, and Calitas, Asrias, and Joazabdus, and Ananias, Biatas, the Levites, taught the law of the Lord, making them withal to understand it. [49] Then spake Attharates unto Esdras the chief priest and reader, and to the Levites that taught the multitude, even to all, saying, [50] This day is holy unto the Lord; (for they all wept when they heard the law:) [51] Go then, and eat the fat, and drink the sweet, and send part to them that have nothing; [52] for this day is holy unto the Lord: and be not sorrowful; for the Lord will bring you to honour. [53] So the Levites published all things to the people, saying, This day is holy to the Lord; be not sorrowful. [54] Then went they their way, every one to eat and drink, and make merry, and to give part to them that had nothing, and to make great cheer; [55] because they understood the words wherein they were instructed, and for the which they had been assembled.

THE SECOND BOOK OF ESDRAS

1 [1] The second book of the prophet Esdras, the son of Saraias, the son of Azarias, the son of Helchias, the son of Sadamias, the son of Sadoc, the son of Achitob, [2] the son of Achias, the son of Phinees, the son of Heli, the son of Amarias, the son of Aziei, the son of Marimoth, the son of Arna, the son of Ozias, the son of Borith, the son of Abisei, the son of Phinees, the son of Eleazar, [3] the son of Aaron, of the tribe of Levi; which was captive in the land of the Medes, in the reign of Artexerxes king of the Persians. [4] And the word of the Lord came unto me, saying, [5] Go thy way, and shew my people their sinful deeds, and their children their wickedness which they have done against me; that they may tell their children's children: [6] Because the sins of their fathers are increased in them: for they have forgotten me, and have offered unto strange gods. [7] Am not I even he that brought them out of the land of Egypt, from the house of bondage? but they have provoked me unto wrath, and despised my counsels. [8] Pull

thou off then the hair of thy head, and cast all evil upon them, for they have not been obedient unto my law, but it is a rebellious people. [9] How long shall I forbear them, unto whom I have done so much good? [10] Many kings have I destroyed for their sakes; Pharaoh with his servants and all his power have I smitten down. [11] All the nations have I destroyed before them, and in the east I have scattered the people of two provinces, even of Tyrus and Sidon, and have slain all their enemies. [12] Speak thou therefore unto them, saying, Thus saith the Lord, [13] I led you through the sea and in the beginning gave you a large and safe passage; I gave you Moses for a leader, and Aaron for a priest. [14] I gave you light in a pillar of fire, and great wonders have I done among you; yet have ye forgotten me, saith the Lord. [15] Thus saith the Almighty Lord, The quails were as a token to you; I gave you tents for your safeguard: nevertheless ye murmured there, [16] and triumphed not in my name for the destruction of your enemies, but ever to this day do ye yet murmur. [17] Where are the benefits that I have done for you? when ye were hungry and thirsty in the wilderness, did ye not cry unto me, [18] saying, Why hast thou brought us into this wilderness to kill us? it had been better for us to have served the Egyptians, than to die in this wilderness. [19] Then had I pity upon your mournings, and gave you manna to eat; so ye did eat angel's bread. [20] When ye were thirsty, did I not cleave the rock, and waters flowed out to your fill? for the heat I covered you with the leaves of the trees. [21] I divided among you a fruitful land, I cast out the Canaanites, the Pherezites, and the Philistines, before you: what shall I yet do more for you? saith the Lord. [22] Thus saith the Almighty Lord, When ye were in the wilderness, in the river of the Amorites, being athirst, and blaspheming my name, [23] I gave you not fire for your blasphemies, but cast a tree in the water, and made the river sweet. [24] What shall I do unto thee, O Jacob? thou, Juda, wouldest not obey me: I will turn me to other nations, and unto those will I give my name, that they may keep my statutes. [25] Seeing ye have forsaken me, I will forsake you also; when ye desire me to be gracious unto you, I shall have no mercy upon you. [26] Whensoever ye shall call upon me, I will not hear you: for ye have defiled your hands with blood, and your feet are swift to commit manslaughter. [27] Ye have not as it were forsaken me, but your own selves, saith the Lord. [28] Thus saith the Almighty Lord, Have I not prayed you as a father his sons, as a mother her daughters, and a nurse her young babes, [29] that ye would be my people, and I should be your God; that ye would be my children, and I should be your father? [30] I gathered you together, as a hen gathereth her chickens under her wings: but now, what shall I do unto you? I will cast you out from my face. [31] When ye offer unto me, I will turn my face from you: for your solemn feastdays, your new moons, and your circumcisions, have I forsaken. [32] I sent unto you my servants the prophets, whom ye have taken and slain, and torn their bodies in pieces, whose blood I will require of your hands, saith the Lord. [33] Thus saith the Almighty Lord, Your house is desolate, I will cast you out as the wind doth stubble. [34] And your children shall not be fruitful; for they have despised my commandment, and done the thing that is evil before me. [35] Your houses will I give to a people that shall come; which not having heard of me yet shall believe me; to whom I have shewed no signs, yet they shall do that I have commanded them. [36] They have seen no prophets, yet they shall call their sins to remembrance, and acknowledge them. [37] I take to witness the grace of the people to come, whose little ones rejoice in gladness: and though they have not seen me with bodily eyes, yet in spirit they believe the thing that I say. [38] And now, brother, behold what glory; and see the people that come from the east: [39] unto whom I will give for leaders, Abraham, Isaac, and Jacob, Oseas, Amos, and Micheas, Joel, Abdias, and Jonas, [40] Nahum, and Abacuc, Sophonias, Aggeus, Zachary, and Malachy, which is called also an angel of the Lord.

2 [1] Thus saith the Lord, I brought this people out of bondage, and I gave them my commandments by my servants the prophets; whom they would not hear, but despised my counsels. [2] The mother that bare them saith unto them, Go your way, ye children; for I am a widow and forsaken. [3] I brought you up with gladness; but with sorrow and heaviness have I lost you: for ye have sinned before the Lord your God, and done that thing that is evil before him. [4] But what shall I now do unto you? I am a widow and forsaken: go your way, O my children, and ask mercy of the Lord. [5] As for me, O father, I call upon thee for a witness over the mother of these children, which would not keep my covenant, [6] that thou bring them to confusion, and their mother to a spoil, that there may be no offspring of them. [7] Let them be scattered abroad among the heathen, let their names be put out of the earth: for they have despised my covenant. [8] Woe be unto thee, Assur, thou that hidest the unrighteous in thee! O thou wicked people, remember what I did unto Sodom and Gomorrah; [9] whose land lieth in clods of pitch and heaps of ashes: even so also will I do unto them that

hear me not, saith the Almighty Lord. [10] Thus saith the Lord unto Esdras, Tell my people that I will give them the kingdom of Jerusalem, which I would have given unto Israel. [11] Their glory also will I take unto me, and give these the everlasting tabernacles, which I had prepared for them. [12] They shall have the tree of life for an ointment of sweet savour; they shall neither labour, nor be weary. [13] Go, and ye shall receive: pray for few days unto you, that they may be shortened: the kingdom is already prepared for you: watch. [14] Take heaven and earth to witness; for I have broken the evil in pieces, and created the good: for I live, saith the Lord. [15] Mother, embrace thy children, and bring them up with gladness, make their feet as fast as a pillar: for I have chosen thee, saith the Lord. [16] And those that be dead will I raise up again from their places, and bring them out of the graves: for I have known my name in Israel. [17] Fear not, thou mother of the children: for I have chosen thee, saith the Lord. [18] For thy help will I send my servants Esau and Jeremy, after whose counsel I have sanctified and prepared for thee twelve trees laden with divers fruits, [19] and as many fountains flowing with milk and honey, and seven mighty mountains, whereupon there grow roses and lilies, whereby I will fill thy children with joy. [20] Do right to the widow, judge for the fatherless, give to the poor, defend the orphan, clothe the naked, [21] heal the broken and the weak, laugh not a lame man to scorn, defend the maimed, and let the blind man come into the sight of my clearness. [22] Keep the old and young within thy walls. [23] Wheresoever thou findest the dead, take them and bury them, and I will give thee the first place in my resurrection. [24] Abide still, O my people, and take thy rest, for thy quietness shall come. [25] Nourish thy children, O thou good nurse; stablish their feet. [26] As for the servants whom I have given thee, there shall not one of them perish; for I will require them from among thy number. [27] Be not weary: for when the day of trouble and heaviness cometh, others shall weep and be sorrowful, but thou shalt be merry and have abundance. [28] The heathen shall envy thee, but they shall be able to do nothing against thee, saith the Lord. [29] My hands shall cover thee, so that thy children shall not see hell. [30] Be joyful, O thou mother, with thy children; for I will deliver thee, saith the Lord. [31] Remember thy children that sleep, for I shall bring them out of the sides of the earth, and shew mercy unto them: for I am merciful, saith the Lord Almighty. [32] Embrace thy children until I come and shew mercy unto them: for my wells run over, and my grace shall not fail. [33] I Esdras received a charge of the Lord upon the mount Oreb, that I should go unto Israel; but when I came unto them, they set me at nought, and despised the commandment of the Lord. [34] And therefore I say unto you, O ye heathen, that hear and understand, look for your Shepherd, he shall give you everlasting rest; for he is nigh at hand, that shall come in the end of the world. [35] Be ready to the reward of the kingdom, for the everlasting light shall shine upon you for evermore. [36] Flee the shadow of this world, receive the joyfulness of your glory: I testify my Saviour openly. [37] O receive the gift that is given you, and be glad, giving thanks unto him that hath called you to the heavenly kingdom. [38] Arise up and stand, behold the number of those that be sealed in the feast of the Lord; [39] which are departed from the shadow of the world, and have received glorious garments of the Lord. [40] Take thy number, O Sion, and shut up those of thine that are clothed in white, which have fulfilled the law of the Lord. [41] The number of thy children, whom thou longedst for, is fulfilled: beseech the power of the Lord, that thy people, which have been called from the beginning, may be hallowed. [42] I Esdras saw upon the mount Sion a great people, whom I could not number, and they all praised the Lord with songs. [43] And in the midst of them there was a young man of a high stature, taller than all the rest, and upon every one of their heads he set crowns, and was more exalted; which I marvelled at greatly. [44] So I asked the angel, and said, Sir, what are these? [45] He answered and said unto me, These be they that have put off the mortal clothing, and put on the immortal, and have confessed the name of God: now are they crowned, and receive palms. [46] Then said I unto the angel, What young person is it that crowneth them, and giveth them palms in their hands? [47] So he answered and said unto me, It is the Son of God, whom they have confessed in the world. Then began I greatly to commend them that stood so stiffly for the name of the Lord. [48] Then the angel said unto me, Go thy way, and tell my people what manner of things, and how great wonders of the Lord thy God, thou hast seen.

3 [1] In the thirtieth year after the ruin of the city, I was in Babylon, and lay troubled upon my bed, and my thoughts came up over my heart: [2] for I saw the desolation of Sion, and the wealth of them that dwelt at Babylon. [3] And my spirit was sore moved, so that I began to speak words full of fear to the most High, and said, [4] O Lord, who bearest rule, thou spakest at the beginning, when thou didst plant the earth, and that thyself alone, and commandedst the people, [5] and gavest a body unto Adam without soul, which was the

workmanship of thine hands, and didst breathe into him the breath of life, and he was made living before thee. [6] And thou leadest him into paradise, which thy right hand had planted, before ever the earth came forward. [7] And unto him thou gavest commandment to love thy way: which he transgressed, and immediately thou appointedst death in him and in his generations, of whom came nations, tribes, people, and kindreds, out of number. [8] And every people walked after their own will, and did wonderful things before thee, and despised thy commandments. [9] And again in process of time thou broughtest the flood upon those that dwelt in the world, and destroyedst them. [10] And it came to pass in every of them, that as death was to Adam, so was the flood to these. [11] Nevertheless one of them thou leftest, namely, Noah with his household, of whom came all righteous men. [12] And it happened, that when they that dwelt upon the earth began to multiply, and had gotten them many children, and were a great people, they began again to be more ungodly than the first. [13] Now when they lived so wickedly before thee, thou didst choose thee a man from among them, whose name was Abraham. [14] Him thou lovedst, and unto him only thou shewedst thy will: [15] And madest an everlasting covenant with him, promising him that thou wouldest never forsake his seed. [16] And unto him thou gavest Isaac, and unto Isaac also thou gavest Jacob and Esau. As for Jacob, thou didst choose him to thee, and put by Esau: and so Jacob became a great multitude. [17] And it came to pass, that when thou leadest his seed out of Egypt, thou broughtest them up to the mount Sinai. [18] And bowing the heavens, thou didst set fast the earth, movedst the whole world, and madest the depths to tremble, and troubledst the men of that age. [19] And thy glory went through four gates, of fire, and of earthquake, and of wind, and of cold; that thou mightest give the law unto the seed of Jacob, and diligence unto the generation of Israel. [20] And yet tookest thou not away from them a wicked heart, that thy law might bring forth fruit in them. [21] For the first Adam bearing a wicked heart transgressed, and was overcome; and so be all they that are born of him. [22] Thus infirmity was made permanent; and the law (also) in the heart of the people with the malignity of the root; so that the good departed away, and the evil abode still. [23] So the times passed away, and the years were brought to an end: then didst thou raise thee up a servant, called David: [24] whom thou commandedst to build a city unto thy name, and to offer incense and oblations unto thee therein. [25] When this was done many years, then they that inhabited the city forsook thee, [26] and in all things did even as Adam and all his generations had done: for they also had a wicked heart: [27] And so thou gavest thy city over into the hands of thine enemies. [28] Are their deeds then any better that inhabit Babylon, that they should therefore have the dominion over Sion? [29] For when I came thither, and had seen impieties without number, then my soul saw many evildoers in this thirtieth year, so that my heart failed me. [30] For I have seen how thou sufferest them sinning, and hast spared wicked doers: and hast destroyed thy people, and hast preserved thine enemies, and hast not signified it. [31] I do not remember how this way may be left: Are they then of Babylon better than they of Sion? [32] Or is there any other people that knoweth thee beside Israel? or what generation hath so believed thy covenants as Jacob? [33] And yet their reward appeareth not, and their labour hath no fruit: for I have gone here and there through the heathen, and I see that they flow in wealth, and think not upon thy commandments. [34] Weigh thou therefore our wickedness now in the balance, and theirs also that dwell in the world; and so shall thy name no where be found but in Israel. [35] Or when was it that they which dwell upon the earth have not sinned in thy sight? or what people have so kept thy commandments? [36] Thou shalt find that Israel by name hath kept thy precepts; but not the heathen.

4 [1] And the angel that was sent unto me, whose name was Uriel, gave me an answer, [2] and said, Thy heart hath gone too far in this world, and thinkest thou to comprehend the way of the most High? [3] Then said I, Yea, my lord. And he answered me, and said, I am sent to shew thee three ways, and to set forth three similitudes before thee: [4] Whereof if thou canst declare me one, I will shew thee also the way that thou desirest to see, and I shall shew thee from whence the wicked heart cometh. [5] And I said, Tell on, my lord. Then said he unto me, Go thy way, weigh me the weight of the fire, or measure me the blast of the wind, or call me again the day that is past. [6] Then answered I and said, What man is able to do that, that thou shouldest ask such things of me? [7] And he said unto me, If I should ask thee how great dwellings are in the midst of the sea, or how many springs are in the beginning of the deep, or how many springs are above the firmament, or which are the outgoings of paradise: [8] Peradventure thou wouldest say unto me, I never went down into the deep, nor as yet into hell, neither did I ever climb up into heaven. [9] Nevertheless now have I asked thee but only of the fire and wind, and of the day wherethrough

thou hast passed, and of things from which thou canst not be separated, and yet canst thou give me no answer of them. [10] He said moreover unto me, Thine own things, and such as are grown up with thee, canst thou not know; [11] how should thy vessel then be able to comprehend the way of the Highest, and, the world being now outwardly corrupted, to understand the corruption that is evident in my sight? [12] Then said I unto him, It were better that we were not at all, than that we should live still in wickedness, and to suffer, and not to know wherefore. [13] He answered me, and said, I went into a forest into a plain, and the trees took counsel, [14] and said, Come, let us go and make war against the sea, that it may depart away before us, and that we may make us more woods. [15] The floods of the sea also in like manner took counsel, and said, Come, let us go up and subdue the woods of the plain, that there also we may make us another country. [16] The thought of the wood was in vain, for the fire came and consumed it. [17] The thought of the floods of the sea came likewise to nought, for the sand stood up and stopped them. [18] If thou wert judge now betwixt these two, whom wouldest thou begin to justify? or whom wouldest thou condemn? [19] I answered and said, Verily it is a foolish thought that they both have devised, for the ground is given unto the wood, and the sea also hath his place to bear his floods. [20] Then answered he me, and said, Thou hast given a right judgment, but why judgest thou not thyself also? [21] For like as the ground is given unto the wood, and the sea to his floods: even so they that dwell upon the earth may understand nothing but that which is upon the earth: and he that dwelleth above the heavens may only understand the things that are above the height of the heavens. [22] Then answered

I and said, I beseech thee, O Lord, let me have understanding: [23] For it was not my mind to be curious of the high things, but of such as pass by us daily, namely, wherefore Israel is given up as a reproach to the heathen, and for what cause the people whom thou hast loved is given over unto ungodly nations, and why the law of our forefathers is brought to nought, and the written covenants come to none effect, [24] and we pass away out of the world as grasshoppers, and our life is astonishment and fear, and we are not worthy to obtain mercy. [25] What will he then do unto his name whereby we are called? of these things have I asked. [26] Then answered he me, and said, The more thou searchest, the more thou shalt marvel; for the world hasteth fast to pass away, [27] and cannot comprehend the things that are promised to the righteous in time to come: for this world is full of unrighteousness and infirmities. [28] But as concerning the things whereof thou askest me, I will tell thee; for the evil is sown, but the destruction thereof is not yet come. [29] If therefore that which is sown be not turned upside down, and if the place where the evil is sown pass not away, then cannot it come that is sown with good. [30] For the grain of evil seed hath been sown in the heart of Adam from the beginning, and how much ungodliness hath it brought up unto this time? and how much shall it yet bring forth until the time of threshing come? [31] Ponder now by thyself, how great fruit of wickedness the grain of evil seed hath brought forth. [32] And when the ears shall be cut down, which are without number, how great a floor shall they fill? [33] Then I answered and said, How, and when shall these things come to pass? wherefore are our years few and evil? [34] And he answered me, saying, Do not thou hasten above the most Highest: for thy haste is in vain to be above him, for thou hast much exceeded. [35] Did not the souls also of the righteous ask question of these things in their chambers, saying, How long shall I hope on this fashion? when cometh the fruit of the floor of our reward? [36] And unto these things Uriel the archangel gave them answer, and said, Even when the number of seeds is filled in you: for he hath weighed the world in the balance. [37] By measure hath he measured the times; and by number hath he numbered the times; and he doth not move nor stir them, until the said measure be fulfilled. [38] Then answered I and said, O Lord that bearest rule, even we all are full of impiety. [39] And for our sakes peradventure it is that the floors of the righteous are not filled, because of the sins of them that dwell upon the earth. [40] So he answered me, and said, Go thy way to a woman with child, and ask of her when she hath fulfilled her nine months, if her womb may keep the birth any longer within her. [41] Then said I, No, Lord, that can she not. And he said unto me, In the grave the chambers of souls are like the womb of a woman: [42] For like as a woman that travaileth maketh haste to escape the necessity of the travail: even so do these places haste to deliver those things that are committed unto them. [43] From the beginning, look, what thou desirest to see, it shall be shewed thee. [44] Then answered I and said, If I have found favour in thy sight, and if it be possible, and if I be meet therefore, [45] shew me then whether there be more to come than is past, or more past than is to come. [46] What is past I know, but what is for to come I know not. [47] And he said unto me, Stand up upon the right side, and I shall expound the similitude unto thee. [48] So I stood, and saw, and, behold, an hot burning oven passed by before me: and it happened that when the flame was gone by I looked, and, behold, the smoke remained still. [49] After this there passed by before me a watery cloud, and sent down much rain with a storm; and when the stormy rain was past, the drops remained still. [50] Then said he unto me, Consider with thyself; as the rain is more than the drops, and as the fire is greater than the smoke; but the drops and the smoke remain behind: so the quantity which is past did more exceed. [51] Then I prayed, and said, May I live, thinkest thou, until that time? or what shall happen in those days? [52] He answered me, and said, As for the tokens whereof thou asketh me, I may tell thee of them in part: but as touching thy life, I am not sent to shew thee; for I do not know it.

5 [1] Nevertheless as concerning the tokens, behold, the days shall come, that they which dwell upon earth shall be taken in a great number, and the way of truth shall be hidden, and the land shall be barren of faith. [2] But iniquity shall be increased above that which now thou seest, or that thou hast heard long ago. [3] And the land, that thou seest now to have root, shalt thou see wasted suddenly. [4] But if the most High grant thee to live, thou shalt see after the third trumpet that the sun shall suddenly shine again in the night, and the moon thrice in the day: [5] And blood shall drop out of wood, and the stone shall give his voice, and the people shall be troubled: [6] And even he shall rule, whom they look not for that dwell upon the earth, and the fowls shall take their flight away together: [7] And the Sodomitish sea shall cast out fish, and make a noise in the night, which many have not known: but they shall all hear the voice thereof. [8] There shall be a confusion also in many places, and the fire shall be oft sent out again, and the wild beasts shall change their places, and menstruous

women shall bring forth monsters: [9] And salt water shall be found in the sweet, and all friends shall destroy one another; then shall wit hide itself, and understanding withdraw itself into his secret chamber, [10] and shall be sought of many, and yet not be found: then shall unrighteousness and incontinency be multiplied upon earth. [11] One land also shall ask another, and say, Is righteousness that maketh a man righteous gone through thee? And it shall say, No. [12] At the same time shall men hope, but nothing obtain: they shall labour, but their ways shall not prosper. [13] To shew thee such tokens I have leave; and if thou wilt pray again, and weep as now, and fast seven days, thou shalt hear yet greater things. [14] Then I awaked, and an extreme fearfulness went through all my body, and my mind was troubled, so that it fainted. [15] So the angel that was come to talk with me held me, comforted me, and set me up upon my feet. [16] And in the second night it came to pass, that Salathiel the captain of the people came unto me, saying, Where hast thou been? and why is thy countenance so heavy? [17] Knowest thou not that Israel is committed unto thee in the land of their captivity? [18] Up then, and eat bread, and forsake us not, as the shepherd that leaveth his flock in the hands of cruel wolves. [19] Then said I unto him, Go thy ways from me, and come not nigh me. And he heard what I said, and went from me. [20] And so I fasted seven days, mourning and weeping, like as Uriel the angel commanded me. [21] And after seven days so it was, that the thoughts of my heart were very grievous unto me again, [22] and my soul recovered the spirit of understanding, and I began to talk with the most High again, [23] and said, O Lord that bearest rule, of every wood of the earth, and of all the trees thereof, thou hast chosen thee one only vine:

[24] And of all lands of the whole world thou hast chosen thee one pit: and of all the flowers thereof one lily: [25] And of all the depths of the sea thou hast filled thee one river: and of all builded cities thou hast hallowed Sion unto thyself: [26] And of all the fowls that are created thou hast named thee one dove: and of all the cattle that are made thou hast provided thee one sheep: [27] And among all the multitudes of people thou hast gotten thee one people: and unto this people, whom thou lovedst, thou gavest a law that is approved of all. [28] And now, O Lord, why hast thou given this one people over unto many? and upon the one root hast thou prepared others, and why hast thou scattered thy only one people among many? [29] And they which did gainsay thy promises, and believed not thy covenants, have trodden them down. [30] If thou didst so much hate thy people, yet shouldest thou punish them with thine own hands. [31] Now when I had spoken these words, the angel that came to me the night afore was sent unto me, [32] and said unto me, Hear me, and I will instruct thee; hearken to the thing that I say, and I shall tell thee more. [33] And I said, Speak on, my Lord. Then said he unto me, Thou art sore troubled in mind for Israel's sake: lovest thou that people better than he that made them? [34] And I said, No, Lord: but of very grief have I spoken: for my reins pain me every hour, while I labour to comprehend the way of the most High, and to seek out part of his judgment. [35] And he said unto me, Thou canst not. And I said, Wherefore, Lord? whereunto was I born then? or why was not my mother's womb then my grave, that I might not have seen the travail of Jacob, and the wearisome toil of the stock of Israel? [36] And he said unto me, Number me the things that are not yet come, gather me together the drops that are

scattered abroad, make me the flowers green again that are withered, [37] open me the places that are closed, and bring me forth the winds that in them are shut up, shew me the image of a voice: and then I will declare to thee the thing that thou labourest to know. [38] And I said, O Lord that bearest rule, who may know these things, but he that hath not his dwelling with men? [39] As for me, I am unwise: how may I then speak of these things whereof thou askest me? [40] Then said he unto me, Like as thou canst do none of these things that I have spoken of, even so canst thou not find out my judgment, or in the end the love that I have promised unto my people. [41] And I said, Behold, O Lord, yet art thou nigh unto them that be reserved till the end: and what shall they do that have been before me, or we that be now, or they that shall come after us? [42] And he said unto me, I will liken my judgment unto a ring: like as there is no slackness of the last, even so there is no swiftness of the first. [43] So I answered and said, Couldest thou not make those that have been made, and be now, and that are for to come, at once; that thou mightest shew thy judgment the sooner? [44] Then answered he me, and said, The creature may not haste above the maker; neither may the world hold them at once that shall be created therein. [45] And I said, As thou hast said unto thy servant, that thou, which givest life to all, hast given life at once to the creature that thou hast created, and the creature bare it: even so it might now also bear them that now be present at once. [46] And he said unto me, Ask the womb of a woman, and say unto her, If thou bringest forth children, why dost thou it not together, but one after another? pray her therefore to bring forth ten children at once. [47] And I said, She cannot: but must do it by distance of time. [48] Then said he unto me, Even so have I given the womb of the earth to those that be sown in it in their times. [49] For like as a young child may not bring forth the things that belong to the aged, even so have I disposed the world which I created. [50] And I asked, and said, Seeing thou hast now given me the way, I will proceed to speak before thee: for our mother, of whom thou hast told me that she is young, draweth now nigh unto age. [51] He answered me, and said, Ask a woman that beareth children, and she shall tell thee. [52] Say unto her, Wherefore are not they whom thou hast now brought forth like those that were before, but less of stature? [53] And she shall answer thee, They that be born in the strength of youth are of one fashion, and they that are born in the time of age, when the womb faileth, are otherwise. [54] Consider thou therefore also, how that ye are less of stature than those that were before you. [55] And so are they that come after you less than ye, as the creatures which now begin to be old, and have passed over the strength of youth. [56] Then said I, Lord, I beseech thee, if I have found favour in thy sight, shew thy servant by whom thou visitest thy creature.

6 [1] And he said unto me, In the beginning, when the earth was made, before the borders of the world stood, or ever the winds blew, [2] before it thundered and lightened, or ever the foundations of paradise were laid, [3] before the fair flowers were seen, or ever the moveable powers were established, before the innumerable multitude of angels were gathered together, [4] or ever the heights of the air were lifted up, before the measures of the firmament were named, or ever the chimneys in Sion were hot, [5] and ere the present years were sought out, and or ever the inventions of them that now sin

were turned, before they were sealed that have gathered faith for a treasure: [6] Then did I consider these things, and they all were made through me alone, and through none other: by me also they shall be ended, and by none other. [7] Then answered I and said, What shall be the parting asunder of the times? or when shall be the end of the first, and the beginning of it that followeth? [8] And he said unto me, From Abraham unto Isaac, when Jacob and Esau were born of him, Jacob's hand held first the heel of Esau. [9] For Esau is the end of the world, and Jacob is the beginning of it that followeth. [10] The hand of man is betwixt the heel and the hand: other question, Esdras, ask thou not. [11] I answered then and said, O Lord that bearest rule, if I have found favour in thy sight, [12] I beseech thee, shew thy servant the end of thy tokens, whereof thou shewedst me part the last night. [13] So he answered and said unto me, Stand up upon thy feet, and hear a mighty sounding voice. [14] And it shall be as it were a great motion; but the place where thou standest shall not be moved. [15] And therefore when it speaketh be not afraid: for the word is of the end, and the foundation of the earth is understood. [16] And why? because the speech of these things trembleth and is moved: for it knoweth that the end of these things must be changed. [17] And it happened, that when I had heard it I stood up upon my feet, and hearkened, and, behold, there was a voice that spake, and the sound of it was like the sound of many waters. [18] And it said, Behold, the day is come, that I will begin to draw nigh, and to visit them that dwell upon the earth, [19] and will begin to make inquisition of them, what they be that have hurt unjustly with their unrighteousness, and when the affliction of Sion shall be fulfilled; [20] and when the world, that shall begin to vanish away, shall be finished, then will I shew these tokens: the books shall be opened before the firmament, and they shall see all together: [21] And the children of a year old shall speak with their voices, the women with child shall bring forth untimely children of three or four months old, and they shall live, and be raised up. [22] And suddenly shall the sown places appear unsown, the full storehouses shall suddenly be found empty: [23] And the trumpet shall give a sound, which when every man heareth, they shall be suddenly afraid. [24] At that time shall friends fight one against another like enemies, and the earth shall stand in fear with those that dwell therein, the springs of the fountains shall stand still, and in three hours they shall not run. [25] Whosoever remaineth from all these that I have told thee shall escape, and see my salvation, and the end of your world. [26] And the men that are received shall see it, who have not tasted death from their birth: and the heart of the inhabitants shall be changed, and turned into another meaning. [27] For evil shall be put out, and deceit shall be quenched. [28] As for faith, it shall flourish, corruption shall be overcome, and the truth, which hath been so long without fruit, shall be declared. [29] And when he talked with me, behold, I looked by little and little upon him before whom I stood. [30] And these words said he unto me; I am come to shew thee the time of the night to come. [31] If thou wilt pray yet more, and fast seven days again, I shall tell thee greater things by day than I have heard. [32] For thy voice is heard before the most High: for the Mighty hath seen thy righteous dealing, he hath seen also thy chastity, which thou hast had ever since thy youth. [33] And therefore hath he sent me to shew thee all these things, and to say unto thee, Be of good comfort and fear not [34] and hasten not with the times that are past, to think vain things, that thou mayest not hasten from the latter times. [35] And it came to pass after this, that I wept again, and fasted seven days in like manner, that I might fulfil the three weeks which he told me. [36] And in the eighth night was my heart vexed within me again, and I began to speak before the most High. [37] For my spirit was greatly set on fire, and my soul was in distress. [38] And I said, O Lord, thou spakest from the beginning of the creation, even the first day, and saidst thus; Let heaven and earth be made; and thy word was a perfect work. [39] And then was the spirit, and darkness and silence were on every side; the sound of man's voice was not yet formed. [40] Then commandedst thou a fair light to come forth of thy treasures, that thy work might appear. [41] Upon the second day thou madest the spirit of the firmament, and commandedst it to part asunder, and to make a division betwixt the waters, that the one part might go up, and the other remain beneath. [42] Upon the third day thou didst command that the waters should be gathered in the seventh part of the earth: six parts hast thou dried up, and kept them, to the intent that of these some being planted of God and tilled might serve thee. [43] For as soon as thy word went forth the work was made. [44] For immediately there was great and innumerable fruit, and many and divers pleasures for the taste, and flowers of unchangeable colour, and odours of wonderful smell: and this was done the third day. [45] Upon the fourth day thou commandedst that the sun should shine, and the moon give her light, and the stars should be in order: [46] And gavest them a charge to do service unto man, that was to be made. [47] Upon the fifth day thou saidst unto the seventh part, where the waters were gathered, that it should bring forth living creatures, fowls and fishes: and so it came to pass. [48] For the dumb water and without life brought forth living things at the commandment of God, that all people might praise thy wondrous works. [49] Then didst thou ordain two living creatures, the one thou calledst Enoch, and the other Leviathan; [50] and didst separate the one from the other: for the seventh part, namely, where the water was gathered together, might not hold them both. [51] Unto Enoch thou gavest one part, which was dried up the third day, that he should dwell in the same part, wherein are a thousand hills: [52] But unto Leviathan thou gavest the seventh part, namely, the moist; and hast kept him to be devoured of whom thou wilt, and when. [53] Upon the sixth day thou gavest commandment unto the earth, that before thee it should bring forth beasts, cattle, and creeping things: [54] And after these, Adam also, whom thou madest lord of all thy creatures: of him come we all, and the people also whom thou hast chosen. [55] All this have I spoken before thee, O Lord, because thou madest the world for our sakes. [56] As for the other people, which also come of Adam, thou hast said that they are nothing, but be like unto spittle: and hast likened the abundance of them unto a drop that falleth from a vessel. [57] And now, O Lord, behold these heathen, which have ever been reputed as nothing, have begun to be lords over us, and to devour us. [58] But we thy people, whom thou hast called thy firstborn, thy only begotten, and thy fervent lover, are given into their hands. [59] If the world now be made for our sakes, why do we not possess an inheritance with the world? how long shall this endure?

7 [1] And when I had made an end of speaking these words, there was sent unto me the angel which had been sent unto me the nights afore: [2] And he said unto me, Up, Esdras, and hear the words that I am come to tell thee. [3] And I said, Speak on, my God. Then said he unto me, The sea is set in a wide place, that it might be deep and great. [4] But put the case the entrance were narrow, and like a river; [5] who then could go into the sea to look upon it, and to rule it? if he went not through the narrow, how could he come into the broad? [6] There is also another thing; a city is builded, and set upon a broad field, and is full of all good things: [7] The entrance thereof is narrow, and is set in a dangerous place to fall, like as if there were a fire on the right hand, and on the left a deep water: [8] And one only path between them both, even between the fire and the water, so small that there could but one man go there at once. [9] If this city now were given unto a man for an inheritance, if he never shall pass the danger set before it, how shall he receive this inheritance? [10] And I said, It is so, Lord. Then said he unto me, Even so also is Israel's portion. [11] Because for their sakes I made the world: and when Adam transgressed my statutes, then was decreed that now is done. [12] Then were the entrances of this world made narrow, full of sorrow and travail: they are but few and evil, full of perils, and very painful. [13] For the entrances of the elder world were wide and sure, and brought immortal fruit. [14] If then they that live labour not to enter these strait and vain things, they can never receive those that are laid up for them. [15] Now therefore why disquietest thou thyself, seeing thou art but a corruptible man? and why art thou moved, whereas thou art but mortal? [16] Why hast thou not considered in thy mind this thing that is to come,

rather than that which is present? [17] Then answered I and said, O Lord that bearest rule, thou hast ordained in thy law, that the righteous should inherit these things, but that the ungodly should perish. [18] Nevertheless the righteous shall suffer strait things, and hope for wide: for they that have done wickedly have suffered the strait things, and yet shall not see the wide. [19] And he said unto me, There is no judge above God, and none that hath understanding above the Highest. [20] For there be many that perish in this life, because they despise the law of God that is set before them. [21] For God hath given strait commandment to such as came, what they should do to live, even as they came, and what they should observe to avoid punishment. [22] Nevertheless they were not obedient unto him; but spake against him, and imagined vain things; [23] and deceived themselves by their wicked deeds; and said of the most High, that he is not; and knew not his ways: [24] But his law have they despised, and denied his covenants; in his statutes have they not been faithful, and have not performed his works. [25] And therefore, Esdras, for the empty are empty things, and for the full are the full things. [26] Behold, the time shall come, that these tokens which I have told thee shall come to pass, and the bride shall appear, and she coming forth shall be seen, that now is withdrawn from the earth. [27] And whosoever is delivered from the foresaid evils shall see my wonders. [28] For my son Jesus shall be revealed with those that be with him, and they that remain shall rejoice within four hundred years. [29] After these years shall my son Christ die, and all men that have life. [30] And the world shall be turned into the old silence seven days, like as in the former judgments: so that no man shall remain. [31] And after seven days the world, that yet awaketh not, shall be raised up, and that shall die that is corrupt [32] and the earth shall restore those that are asleep in her, and so shall the dust those that dwell in silence, and the secret places shall deliver those souls that were committed unto them. [33] And the most High shall appear upon the seat of judgment, and misery shall pass away, and the long suffering shall have an end: [34] But judgment only shall remain, truth shall stand, and faith shall wax strong: [35] And the work shall follow, and the reward shall be shewed, and the good deeds shall be of force, and wicked deeds shall bear no rule. [36] Then said I, Abraham prayed first for the Sodomites, and Moses for the fathers that sinned in the wilderness: [37] and Jesus after him for Israel in the time of Achan: [38] and Samuel and David for the destruction: and Solomon for them that should come to the sanctuary: [39] and Helias for those that received rain; and for the dead, that he might live: [40] and Ezechias for the people in the time of Sennacherib: and many for many. [41] Even so now, seeing corruption is grown up, and wickedness increased, and the righteous have prayed for the ungodly: wherefore shall it not be so now also? [42] He answered me, and said, This present life is not the end where much glory doth abide; therefore have they prayed for the weak. [43] But the day of doom shall be the end of this time, and the beginning of the immortality for to come, wherein corruption is past, [44] intemperance is at an end, infidelity is cut off, righteousness is grown, and truth is sprung up. [45] Then shall no man be able to save him that is destroyed, nor to oppress him that hath gotten the victory. [46] I answered then and said, This is my first and last saying, that it had been better not to have given the earth unto Adam: or else, when it was given him, to have restrained him from sinning. [47] For what profit is it for men now in this present time to live in heaviness, and after death to look for punishment? [48] O thou Adam, what hast thou done? for though it was thou that sinned, thou art not fallen alone, but we all that come of thee. [49] For what profit is it unto us, if there be promised us an immortal time, whereas we have done the works that bring death? [50] And that there is promised us an everlasting hope, whereas ourselves being most wicked are made vain? [51] And that there are laid up for us dwellings of health and safety, whereas we have lived wickedly? [52] And that the glory of the most High is kept to defend them which have led a wary life, whereas we have walked in the most wicked ways of all? [53] And that there should be shewed a paradise, whose fruit endureth for ever, wherein is security and medicine, since we shall not enter into it? [54] (For we have walked in unpleasant places.) [55] And that the faces of them which have used abstinence shall shine above the stars, whereas our faces shall be blacker than darkness? [56] For while we lived and committed iniquity, we considered not that we should begin to suffer for it after death. [57] Then answered he me, and said, This is the condition of the battle, which man that is born upon the earth shall fight; [58] that, if he be overcome, he shall suffer as thou hast said: but if he get the victory, he shall receive the thing that I say. [59] For this is the life whereof Moses spake unto the people while he lived, saying, Choose thee life, that thou mayest live. [60] Nevertheless they believed not him, nor yet the prophets after him, no, nor me which have spoken unto them, [61] that there should not be such heaviness in their destruction, as shall be joy over them that are persuaded to salvation. [62] I answered then, and said, I know, Lord, that the most High is called merciful, in that he hath mercy upon them which are not yet come into the world, [63] and upon those also that turn to his law; [64] and that he is patient, and long suffereth those that have sinned, as his creatures; [65] and that he is bountiful, for he is ready to give where it needeth; [66] and that he is of great mercy, for he multiplieth more and more mercies to them that are present, and that are past, and also to them which are to come. [67] For if he shall not multiply his mercies, the world would not continue with them that inherit therein. [68] And he pardoneth; for if he did not so of his goodness, that they which have committed iniquities might be eased of them, the ten thousandth part of men should not remain living. [69] And being judge, if he should not forgive them that are cured with his word, and put out the multitude of contentions, [70] there should be very few left peradventure in an innumerable multitude.

8 [1] And he answered me, saying, The most High hath made this world for many, but the world to come for few. [2] I will tell thee a similitude, Esdras; As when thou askest the earth, it shall say unto thee, that it giveth much mould whereof earthen vessels are made, but little dust that gold cometh of: even so is the course of this present world. [3] There be many created, but few shall be saved. [4] So answered I and said, Swallow then down, O my soul, understanding, and devour wisdom. [5] For thou hast agreed to give ear, and art willing to prophesy: for thou hast no longer space than only to live. [6] O Lord, if thou suffer not thy servant, that we may pray before thee, and thou give us seed unto our heart, and culture to our understanding, that there may come fruit of it; how shall each man live that is corrupt,

who beareth the place of a man? [7] For thou art alone, and we all one workmanship of thine hands, like as thou hast said. [8] For when the body is fashioned now in the mother's womb, and thou givest it members, thy creature is preserved in fire and water, and nine months doth thy workmanship endure thy creature which is created in her. [9] But that which keepeth and is kept shall both be preserved: and when the time cometh, the womb preserved delivereth up the things that grew in it. [10] For thou hast commanded out of the parts of the body, that is to say, out of the breasts, milk to be given, which is the fruit of the breasts, [11] that the thing which is fashioned may be nourished for a time, till thou disposest it to thy mercy. [12] Thou broughtest it up with thy righteousness, and nurturedst it in thy law, and reformedst it with thy judgment. [13] And thou shalt mortify it as thy creature, and quicken it as thy work. [14] If therefore thou shalt destroy him which with so great labour was fashioned, it is an easy thing to be ordained by thy commandment, that the thing which was made might be preserved. [15] Now therefore, Lord, I will speak; touching man in general, thou knowest best; but touching thy people, for whose sake I am sorry; [16] and for thine inheritance, for whose cause I mourn; and for Israel, for whom I am heavy; and for Jacob, for whose sake I am troubled; [17] therefore will I begin to pray before thee for myself and for them: for I see the falls of us that dwell in the land. [18] But I have heard the swiftness of the judge which is to come. [19] Therefore hear my voice, and understand my words, and I shall speak before thee. This is the beginning of the words of Esdras, before he was taken up: and I said, [20] O Lord, thou that dwellest in everlastingness which beholdest from above things in the heaven and in the air; [21] whose throne is inestimable; whose glory may not be comprehended; before whom the hosts of angels stand with trembling, [22] whose service is conversant in wind and fire; whose word is true, and sayings constant; whose commandment is strong, and ordinance fearful; [23] whose look drieth up the depths, and indignation maketh the mountains to melt away; which the truth witnesseth: [24] O hear the prayer of thy servant, and give ear to the petition of thy creature. [25] For while I live I will speak, and so long as I have understanding I will answer. [26] O look not upon the sins of thy people; but on them which serve thee in truth. [27] Regard not the wicked inventions of the heathen, but the desire of those that keep thy testimonies in afflictions. [28] Think not upon those that have walked feignedly before thee: but remember them, which according to thy will have known thy fear. [29] Let it not be thy will to destroy them which have lived like beasts; but to look upon them that have clearly taught thy law. [30] Take thou no indignation at them which are deemed worse than beasts; but love them that always put their trust in thy righteousness and glory. [31] For we and our fathers do languish of such diseases: but because of us sinners thou shalt be called merciful. [32] For if thou hast a desire to have mercy upon us, thou shalt be called merciful, to us namely, that have no works of righteousness. [33] For the just, which have many good works laid up with thee, shall out of their own deeds receive reward. [34] For what is man, that thou shouldest take displeasure at him? or what is a corruptible generation, that thou shouldest be so bitter toward it? [35] For in truth there is no man among them that be born, but he hath dealt wickedly; and among the faithful there is none which hath not done amiss. [36] For in this, O Lord, thy righteousness and thy goodness shall be declared, if thou be merciful unto them which have not the confidence of good works. [37] Then answered he me, and said, Some things hast thou spoken aright, and according unto thy words it shall be. [38] For indeed I will not think on the disposition of them which have sinned before death, before judgment, before destruction: [39] But I will rejoice over the disposition of the righteous, and I will remember also their pilgrimage, and the salvation, and the reward, that they shall have. [40] Like as I have spoken now, so shall it come to pass. [41] For as the husbandman soweth much seed upon the ground, and planteth many trees, and yet the thing that is sown good in his season cometh not up, neither doth all that is planted take root: even so is it of them that are sown in the world; they shall not all be saved. [42] I answered then and said, If I have found grace, let me speak. [43] Like as the husbandman's seed perisheth, if it come not up, and receive not thy rain in due season; or if there come too much rain, and corrupt it: [44] even so perisheth man also, which is formed with thy hands, and is called thine own image, because thou art like unto him, for whose sake thou hast made all things, and likened him unto the husbandman's seed. [45] Be not wroth with us but spare thy people, and have mercy upon thine own inheritance: for thou art merciful unto thy creature. [46] Then answered he me, and said, Things present are for the present, and things to come for such as be to come. [47] For thou comest far short that thou shouldest be able to love my creature more than I: but I have ofttimes drawn nigh unto thee, and unto it, but never to the unrighteous. [48] In this also thou art marvellous before the most High: [49] in that thou hast humbled thyself, as it becometh thee, and hast not judged thyself worthy to be much glorified among the righteous. [50] For many great miseries shall be done to them that in the latter time shall dwell in the world, because they have walked in great pride. [51] But understand thou for thyself, and seek out the glory for such as be like thee. [52] For unto you is paradise opened, the tree of life is planted, the time to come is prepared, plenteousness is made ready, a city is builded, and rest is allowed, yea, perfect goodness and wisdom. [53] The root of evil is sealed up from you, weakness and the moth is hid from you, and corruption is fled into hell to be forgotten: [54] Sorrows are passed, and in the end is shewed the treasure of immortality. [55] And therefore ask thou no more questions concerning the multitude of them that perish. [56] For when they had taken liberty, they despised the most High, thought scorn of his law, and forsook his ways. [57] Moreover they have trodden down his righteous, [58] and said in their heart, that there is no God; yea, and that knowing they must die. [59] For as the things aforesaid shalt receive you, so thirst and pain are prepared for them: for it was not his will that men should come to naught: [60] But they which he created have defiled the name of him that made them, and were unthankful unto him which prepared life for them. [61] And therefore is my judgment now at hand. [62] These things have I not shewed unto all men, but unto thee, and a few like thee. Then answered I and said, [63] Behold, O Lord, now hast thou shewed me the multitude of the wonders, which thou wilt begin to do in the last times: but at what time, thou hast not shewed me.

9 [1] He answered me then, and said, Measure thou the time diligently in itself: and when thou seest part of the

signs past, which I have told thee before, [2] then shalt thou understand, that it is the very same time, wherein the Highest will begin to visit the world which he made. [3] Therefore when there shall be seen earthquakes and uproars of the people in the world: [4] Then shalt thou well understand, that the most High spake of those things from the days that were before thee, even from the beginning. [5] For like as all that is made in the world hath a beginning and an end, and the end is manifest: [6] even so the times also of the Highest have plain beginnings in wonder and powerful works, and endings in effects and signs. [7] And every one that shall be saved, and shall be able to escape by his works, and by faith, whereby ye have believed, [8] shall be preserved from the said perils, and shall see my salvation in my land, and within my borders: for I have sanctified them for me from the beginning. [9] Then shall they be in pitiful case, which now have abused my ways: and they that have cast them away despitefully shall dwell in torments. [10] For such as in their life have received benefits, and have not known me; [11] and they that have loathed my law, while they had yet liberty, and, when as yet place of repentance was open unto them, understood not, but despised it; [12] the same must know it after death by pain. [13] And therefore be thou not curious how the ungodly shall be punished, and when: but enquire how the righteous shall be saved, whose the world is, and for whom the world is created. [14] Then answered I and said, [15] I have said before, and now do speak, and will speak it also hereafter, that there be many more of them which perish, than of them which shall be saved: [16] like as a wave is greater than a drop. [17] And he answered me, saying, Like as the field is, so is also the seed; as the flowers be, such are the colours also; such as the workman is, such also is the work; and as the husbandman is himself, so is his husbandry also: for it was the time of the world. [18] And now when I prepared the world, which was not yet made, even for them to dwell in that now live, no man spake against me. [19] For then every one obeyed: but now the manners of them which are created in this world that is made are corrupted by a perpetual seed, and by a law which is unsearchable rid themselves. [20] So I considered the world, and, behold, there was peril because of the devices that were come into it. [21] And I saw, and spared it greatly, and have kept me a grape of the cluster, and a plant of a great people. [22] Let the multitude perish then, which was born in vain; and let my grape be kept, and my plant; for with great labour have I made it perfect. [23] Nevertheless, if thou wilt cease yet seven days more (but thou shalt not fast in them, [24] but go into a field of flowers, where no house is builded, and eat only the flowers of the field; taste no flesh, drink no wine, but eat flowers only;) [25] and pray unto the Highest continually, then will I come and talk with thee. [26] So I went my way into the field which is called Ardath, like as he commanded me; and there I sat among the flowers, and did eat of the herbs of the field, and the meat of the same satisfied me. [27] After seven days I sat upon the grass, and my heart was vexed within me, like as before: [28] And I opened my mouth, and began to talk before the most High, and said, [29] O Lord, thou that shewest thyself unto us, thou wast shewed unto our fathers in the wilderness, in a place where no man treadeth, in a barren place, when they came out of Egypt. [30] And thou spakest saying, Hear me, O Israel; and mark my words, thou seed of Jacob. [31] For, behold, I sow my law in you, and it shall bring fruit in you, and ye shall be honoured in it for ever. [32] But our fathers, which received the law, kept it not, and observed not thine ordinances: and though the fruit of thy law did not perish, neither could it, for it was thine; [33] yet they that received it perished, because they kept not the thing that was sown in them. [34] And, lo, it is a custom, when the ground hath received seed, or the sea a ship, or any vessel meat or drink, that, that being perished wherein it was sown or cast into, [35] that thing also which was sown, or cast therein, or received, doth perish, and remaineth not with us: but with us it hath not happened so. [36] For we that have received the law perish by sin, and our heart also which received it [37] notwithstanding the law perisheth not, but remaineth in his force. [38] And when I spake these things in my heart, I looked back with mine eyes, and upon the right side I saw a woman, and, behold, she mourned and wept with a loud voice, and was much grieved in heart, and her clothes were rent, and she had ashes upon her head. [39] Then let I my thoughts go that I was in, and turned me unto her, [40] and said unto her, Wherefore weepest thou? why art thou so grieved in thy mind? [41] And she said unto me, Sir, let me alone, that I may bewail myself, and add unto my sorrow, for I am sore vexed in my mind, and brought very low. [42] And I said unto her, What aileth thee? tell me. [43] She said unto me, I thy servant have been barren, and had no child, though I had an husband thirty years, [44] and those thirty years I did nothing else day and night, and every hour, but make my prayer to the Highest. [45] After thirty years God heard me thine handmaid, looked upon my misery, considered my trouble, and gave me a son: and I was very glad of him, so was my husband also, and all my neighbours: and we gave great honour unto the

Almighty. [46] And I nourished him with great travail. [47] So when he grew up, and came to the time that he should have a wife, I made a feast.

10 [1] And it so came to pass, that when my son was entered into his wedding chamber, he fell down, and died. [2] Then we all overthrew the lights, and all my neighbours rose up to comfort me: so I took my rest unto the second day at night. [3] And it came to pass, when they had all left off to comfort me, to the end I might be quiet; then rose I up by night and fled, and came hither into this field, as thou seest. [4] And I do now purpose not to return into the city, but here to stay, and neither to eat nor drink, but continually to mourn and to fast until I die. [5] Then left I the meditations wherein I was, and spake to her in anger, saying, [6] Thou foolish woman above all other, seest thou not our mourning, and what happeneth unto us? [7] How that Sion our mother is full of all heaviness, and much humbled, mourning very sore? [8] And now, seeing we all mourn and are sad, for we are all in heaviness, art thou grieved for one son? [9] For ask the earth, and she shall tell thee, that it is she which ought to mourn for the fall of so many that grow upon her. [10] For out of her came all at the first, and out of her shall all others come, and, behold, they walk almost all into destruction, and a multitude of them is utterly rooted out. [11] Who then should make more mourning than she, that hath lost so great a multitude; and not thou, which art sorry but for one? [12] But if thou sayest unto me, My lamentation is not like the earth's, because I have lost the fruit of my womb, which I brought forth with pains, and bare with sorrows; [13] but the earth not so: for the multitude present in it according to the course of the earth is gone,

as it came: [14] Then say I unto thee, Like as thou hast brought forth with labour; even so the earth also hath given her fruit, namely, man, ever since the beginning unto him that made her. [15] Now therefore keep thy sorrow to thyself, and bear with a good courage that which hath befallen thee. [16] For if thou shalt acknowledge the determination of God to be just, thou shalt both receive thy son in time, and shalt be commended among women. [17] Go thy way then into the city to thine husband. [18] And she said unto me, That will I not do: I will not go into the city, but here will I die. [19] So I proceeded to speak further unto her, and said, [20] Do not so, but be counselled by me: for how many are the adversities of Sion? be comforted in regard of the sorrow of Jerusalem. [21] For thou seest that our sanctuary is laid waste, our altar broken down, our temple destroyed; [22] our psaltery is laid on the ground, our song is put to silence, our rejoicing is at an end, the light of our candlestick is put out, the ark of our covenant is spoiled, our holy things are defiled, and the name that is called upon us is almost profaned: our children are put to shame, our priests are burnt, our Levites are gone into captivity, our virgins are defiled, and our wives ravished; our righteous men carried away, our little ones destroyed, our young men are brought in bondage, and our strong men are become weak; [23] and, which is the greatest of all, the seal of Sion hath now lost her honour; for she is delivered into the hands of them that hate us. [24] And therefore shake off thy great heaviness, and put away the multitude of sorrows, that the Mighty may be merciful unto thee again, and the Highest shall give thee rest and ease from thy labour. [25] And it came to pass while I was talking with her, behold, her face upon a sudden shined exceedingly, and her countenance glistered, so that I was afraid of her, and mused what it might be. [26] And, behold, suddenly she made a great cry, very fearful: so that the earth shook at the noise of the woman. [27] And I looked, and, behold, the woman appeared unto me no more, but there was a city builded, and a large place shewed itself from the foundations: then was I afraid, and cried with a loud voice, and said, [28] Where is Uriel the angel, who came unto me at the first? for he hath caused me to fall into many trances, and mine end is turned into corruption, and my prayer to rebuke. [29] And as I was speaking these words behold, he came unto me, and looked upon me. [30] And, lo, I lay as one that had been dead, and mine understanding was taken from me: and he took me by the right hand, and comforted me, and set me upon my feet, and said unto me, [31] What aileth thee? and why art thou so disquieted? and why is thine understanding troubled, and the thoughts of thine heart? [32] And I said, Because thou hast forsaken me, and yet I did according to thy words, and I went into the field, and, lo, I have seen, and yet see, that I am not able to express. [33] And he said unto me, Stand up manfully, and I will advise thee. [34] Then said I, Speak on, my lord, in me; only forsake me not, lest I die frustrate of my hope. [35] For I have seen that I knew not, and hear that I do not know. [36] Or is my sense deceived, or my soul in a dream? [37] Now therefore I beseech thee that thou wilt shew thy servant of this vision. [38] He answered me then, and said, Hear me, and I shall inform thee, and tell thee wherefore thou art afraid: for the Highest will reveal many secret things unto thee. [39] He hath seen that thy way is right: for that thou sorrowest continually for thy people, and makest great lamentation for Sion. [40] This therefore is the meaning of the vision which thou lately sawest: [41] Thou sawest a woman mourning, and thou begannest to comfort her: [42] But now seest thou the likeness of the woman no more, but there appeared unto thee a city builded. [43] And whereas she told thee of the death of her son, this is the solution: [44] This woman, whom thou sawest is Sion: and whereas she said unto thee, even she whom thou seest as a city builded, [45] whereas, I say, she said unto thee, that she hath been thirty years barren: those are the thirty years wherein there was no offering made in her. [46] But after thirty years Solomon builded the city and offered offerings: and then bare the barren a son. [47] And whereas she told thee that she nourished him with labour: that was the dwelling in Jerusalem. [48] But whereas she said unto thee, That my son coming into his marriage chamber happened to have a fall, and died: this was the destruction that came to Jerusalem. [49] And, behold, thou sawest her likeness, and because she mourned for her son, thou begannest to comfort her: and of these things which have chanced, these are to be opened unto thee. [50] For now the most High seeth that thou art grieved unfeignedly, and sufferest from thy whole heart for her, so hath he shewed thee the brightness of her glory, and the comeliness of her beauty: [51] And therefore I bade thee remain in the field where no house was builded: [52] For I knew that the Highest would shew this unto thee. [53] Therefore I commanded thee to go into the field, where no foundation of any building was. [54] For in the place wherein the Highest beginneth to shew his city, there can no man's building be able to stand. [55] And therefore fear not, let not thine heart be affrighted, but go thy way in, and see the beauty and greatness of the building, as much as thine eyes be able to see: [56] And then shalt thou hear as much as thine ears may comprehend. [57] For thou art blessed above many other, and art called with the Highest; and so are but few. [58] But to morrow at night thou shalt remain here; [59] and so shall the Highest shew thee visions of the high things, which the most High will do unto them that dwell upon the earth in the last days. So I slept that night and another, like as he commanded me.

11

[1] Then saw I a dream, and, behold, there came up from the sea an eagle, which had twelve feathered wings, and three heads. [2] And I saw, and, behold, she spread her wings over all the earth, and all the winds of the air blew on her, and were gathered together. [3] And I beheld, and out of her feathers there grew other contrary feathers; and they became little feathers and small. [4] But her heads were at rest: the head in the midst was greater than the other, yet rested it with the residue. [5] Moreover I beheld, and, lo, the eagle flew with her feathers, and reigned upon earth, and over them that dwelt therein. [6] And I saw that all things under heaven were subject unto her, and no man spake against her, no, not one creature upon earth. [7] And I beheld, and, lo, the eagle rose upon her talons, and spake to her feathers, saying, [8] Watch not all at once: sleep every one in his own place, and watch by course: [9] but let the heads be preserved for the last. [10] And I beheld, and, lo, the voice went not out of her heads, but from the midst of her body. [11] And I numbered her contrary feathers, and, behold, there were eight of them. [12] And I looked, and, behold, on the right side there arose one feather, and reigned over all the earth; [13] and so it was, that when it reigned, the end of it came, and the place thereof appeared no more: so the

next following stood up and reigned, and had a great time; [14] and it happened, that when it reigned, the end of it came also, like as the first, so that it appeared no more. [15] Then came there a voice unto it, and said, [16] Hear thou that hast borne rule over the earth so long: this I say unto thee, before thou beginnest to appear no more, [17] there shall none after thee attain unto thy time, neither unto the half thereof. [18] Then arose the third, and reigned as the other before, and appeared no more also. [19] So went it with all the residue one after another, as that every one reigned, and then appeared no more. [20] Then I beheld, and, lo, in process of time the feathers that followed stood up upon the right side, that they might rule also; and some of them ruled, but within a while they appeared no more: [21] for some of them were set up, but ruled not. [22] After this I looked, and, behold, the twelve feathers appeared no more, nor the two little feathers: [23] and there was no more upon the eagle's body, but three heads that rested, and six little wings. [24] Then saw I also that two little feathers divided themselves from the six, and remained under the head that was upon the right side: for the four continued in their place. [25] And I beheld, and, lo, the feathers that were under the wing thought to set up themselves and to have the rule. [26] And I beheld, and, lo, there was one set up, but shortly it appeared no more. [27] And the second was sooner away than the first. [28] And I beheld, and, lo, the two that remained thought also in themselves to reign: [29] and when they so thought, behold, there awaked one of the heads that were at rest, namely, it that was in the midst; for that was greater than the two other heads. [30] And then I saw that the two other heads were joined with it. [31] And, behold, the head was turned with them that were with it, and did eat up the two feathers under the wing that would have reigned. [32] But this head put the whole earth in fear, and bare rule in it over all those that dwelt upon the earth with much oppression; and it had the governance of the world more than all the wings that had been. [33] And after this I beheld, and, lo, the head that was in the midst suddenly appeared no more, like as the wings. [34] But there remained the two heads, which also in like sort ruled upon the earth, and over those that dwelt therein. [35] And I beheld, and, lo, the head upon the right side devoured it that was upon the left side. [36] Then I heard a voice, which said unto me, Look before thee, and consider the thing that thou seest. [37] And I beheld, and lo, as it were a roaring lion chased out of the wood: and I saw that he sent out a man's voice unto the eagle, and said, [38] Hear thou, I will talk with thee, and the Highest shall say unto thee, [39] Art not thou it that remainest of the four beasts, whom I made to reign in my world, that the end of their times might come through them? [40] And the fourth came, and overcame all the beasts that were past, and had power over the world with great fearfulness, and over the whole compass of the earth with much wicked oppression; and so long time dwelt he upon the earth with deceit. [41] For the earth hast thou not judged with truth. [42] For thou hast afflicted the meek, thou hast hurt the peaceable, thou hast loved liars, and destroyed the dwellings of them that brought forth fruit, and hast cast down the walls of such as did thee no harm. [43] Therefore is thy wrongful dealing come up unto the Highest, and thy pride unto the Mighty. [44] The Highest also hath looked upon the proud times, and, behold, they are ended, and his abominations are fulfilled. [45] And therefore appear no more, thou eagle, nor thy horrible wings, nor thy wicked feathers, nor thy malicious heads, nor thy hurtful claws, nor all thy vain body: [46] That all the earth may be refreshed, and may return, being delivered from thy violence, and that she may hope for the judgment and mercy of him that made her.

12 [1] And it came to pass, while the lion spake these words unto the eagle, I saw, [2] and, behold, the head that remained and the four wings appeared no more, and the two went unto it and set themselves up to reign, and their kingdom was small, and full of uproar. [3] And I saw, and, behold, they appeared no more, and the whole body of the eagle was burnt so that the earth was in great fear: then awaked I out of the trouble and trance of my mind, and from great fear, and said unto my spirit, [4] Lo, this hast thou done unto me, in that thou searchest out the ways of the Highest. [5] Lo, yet am I weary in my mind, and very weak in my spirit; and little strength is there in me, for the great fear wherewith I was afflicted this night. [6] Therefore will I now beseech the Highest, that he will comfort me unto the end. [7] And I said, Lord that bearest rule, if I have found grace before thy sight, and if I am justified with thee before many others, and if my prayer indeed be come up before thy face; [8] comfort me then, and shew me thy servant the interpretation and plain difference of this fearful vision, that thou mayest perfectly comfort my soul. [9] For thou hast judged me worthy to shew me the last times. [10] And he said unto me, This is the interpretation of the vision: [11] The eagle, whom thou sawest come up from the sea, is the kingdom which was seen in the vision of thy brother Daniel. [12] But it was not expounded unto him, therefore now I declare it unto

thee. [13] Behold, the days will come, that there shall rise up a kingdom upon earth, and it shall be feared above all the kingdoms that were before it. [14] In the same shall twelve kings reign, one after another: [15] whereof the second shall begin to reign, and shall have more time than any of the twelve. [16] And this do the twelve wings signify, which thou sawest. [17] As for the voice which thou heardest speak, and that thou sawest not to go out from the heads but from the midst of the body thereof, this is the interpretation: [18] That after the time of that kingdom there shall arise great strivings, and it shall stand in peril of falling: nevertheless it shall not then fall, but shall be restored again to his beginning. [19] And whereas thou sawest the eight small under feathers sticking to her wings, this is the interpretation: [20] That in him there shall arise eight kings, whose times shall be but small, and their years swift. [21] And two of them shall perish, the middle time approaching: four shall be kept until their end begin to approach: but two shall be kept unto the end. [22] And whereas thou sawest three heads resting, this is the interpretation: [23] In his last days shall the most High raise up three kingdoms, and renew many things therein, and they shall have the dominion of the earth, [24] and of those that dwell therein, with much oppression, above all those that were before them: therefore are they called the heads of the eagle. [25] For these are they that shall accomplish his wickedness, and that shall finish his last end. [26] And whereas thou sawest that the great head appeared no more, it signifieth that one of them shall die upon his bed, and yet with pain. [27] For the two that remain shall be slain with the sword. [28] For the sword of the one shall devour the other: but at the last shall he fall through the sword himself. [29] And whereas thou sawest two feathers under the wings passing over the head that is on the right side; [30] it signifieth that these are they whom the Highest hath kept unto their end: this is the small kingdom and full of trouble, as thou sawest. [31] And the lion, whom thou sawest rising up out of the wood, and roaring, and speaking to the eagle, and rebuking her for her unrighteousness with all the words which thou hast heard; [32] this is the anointed, which the Highest hath kept for them and for their wickedness unto the end: he shall reprove them, and shall upbraid them with their cruelty. [33] For he shall set them before him alive in judgment, and shall rebuke them, and correct them. [34] For the rest of my people shall he deliver with mercy, those that have been pressed upon my borders, and he shall make them joyful until the coming of the day of judgment, whereof I have spoken unto thee from the beginning. [35] This is the dream that thou sawest, and these are the interpretations. [36] Thou only hast been meet to know this secret of the Highest. [37] Therefore write all these things that thou hast seen in a book, and hide them: [38] And teach them to the wise of the people, whose hearts thou knowest may comprehend and keep these secrets. [39] But wait thou here thyself yet seven days more, that it may be shewed thee, whatsoever it pleaseth the Highest to declare unto thee. And with that he went his way. [40] And it came to pass, when all the people saw that the seven days were past, and I not come again into the city, they gathered them all together, from the least unto the greatest, and came unto me, and said, [41] What have we offended thee? and what evil have we done against thee, that thou forsakest us, and sittest here in this place? [42] For of all the prophets thou only art left us, as a cluster of the vintage, and as a candle in a dark place, and as a haven or ship preserved from the tempest. [43] Are not the evils which are come to us sufficient? [44] If thou shalt forsake us, how much better had it been for us, if we also had been burned in the midst of Sion? [45] For we are not better than they that died there. And they wept with a loud voice. Then answered I them, and said, [46] Be of good comfort, O Israel; and be not heavy, thou house of Jacob: [47] For the Highest hath you in remembrance, and the Mighty hath not forgotten you in temptation. [48] As for me, I have not forsaken you, neither am I departed from you: but am come into this place, to pray for the desolation of Sion, and that I might seek mercy for the low estate of your sanctuary. [49] And now go your way home every man, and after these days will I come unto you. [50] So the people went their way into the city, like as I commanded them: [51] but I remained still in the field seven days, as the angel commanded me; and did eat only in those days of the flowers of the field, and had my meat of the herbs.

13 [1] And it came to pass after seven days, I dreamed a dream by night: [2] And, lo, there arose a wind from the sea, that it moved all the waves thereof. [3] And I beheld, and, lo, that man waxed strong with the thousands of heaven: and when he turned his countenance to look, all the things trembled that were seen under him. [4] And whensoever the voice went out of his mouth, all they burned that heard his voice, like as the earth faileth when it feeleth the fire. [5] And after this I beheld, and, lo, there was gathered together a multitude of men, out of number, from the four winds of the heaven, to subdue the man that came out of the sea [6] but I beheld, and, lo, he had graved himself a great mountain, and flew up upon it. [7] But I would have seen

the region or place whereout the hill was graven, and I could not. [8] And after this I beheld, and, lo, all they which were gathered together to subdue him were sore afraid, and yet durst fight. [9] And, lo, as he saw the violence of the multitude that came, he neither lifted up his hand, nor held sword, nor any instrument of war: [10] But only I saw that he sent out of his mouth as it had been a blast of fire, and out of his lips a flaming breath, and out of his tongue he cast out sparks and tempests. [11] And they were all mixed together; the blast of fire, the flaming breath, and the great tempest; and fell with violence upon the multitude which was prepared to fight, and burned them up every one, so that upon a sudden of an innumerable multitude nothing was to be perceived, but only dust and smell of smoke: when I saw this I was afraid. [12] Afterward saw I the same man come down from the mountain, and call unto him another peaceable multitude. [13] And there came much people unto him, whereof some were glad, some were sorry, and some of them were bound, and other some brought of them that were offered: then was I sick through great fear, and I awaked, and said, [14] Thou hast shewed thy servant these wonders from the beginning, and hast counted me worthy that thou shouldest receive my prayer: [15] Shew me now yet the interpretation of this dream. [16] For as I conceive in mine understanding, woe unto them that shall be left in those days and much more woe unto them that are not left behind! [17] For they that were not left were in heaviness. [18] Now understand I the things that are laid up in the latter days, which shall happen unto them, and to those that are left behind. [19] Therefore are they come into great perils and many necessities, like as these dreams declare. [20] Yet is it easier for him that is in danger to come into these things, than to pass away as a cloud out of the world, and not to see the things that happen in the last days. And he answered unto me, and said, [21] The interpretation of the vision shall I shew thee, and I will open unto thee the thing that thou hast required. [22] Whereas thou hast spoken of them that are left behind, this is the interpretation: [23] He that shall endure the peril in that time hath kept himself: they that be fallen into danger are such as have works, and faith toward the Almighty. [24] Know this therefore, that they which be left behind are more blessed than they that be dead. [25] This is the meaning of the vision: Whereas thou sawest a man coming up from the midst of the sea: [26] the same is he whom God the Highest hath kept a great season, which by his own self shall deliver his creature: and he shall order them that are left behind. [27] And whereas thou sawest, that out of his mouth there came as a blast of wind, and fire, and storm; [28] and that he held neither sword, nor any instrument of war, but that the rushing in of him destroyed the whole multitude that came to subdue him; this is the interpretation: [29] Behold, the days come, when the most High will begin to deliver them that are upon the earth. [30] And he shall come to the astonishment of them that dwell on the earth. [31] And one shall undertake to fight against another, one city against another, one place against another, one people against another, and one realm against another. [32] And the time shall be when these things shall come to pass, and the signs shall happen which I shewed thee before, and then shall my Son be declared, whom thou sawest as a man ascending. [33] And when all the people hear his voice, every man shall in their own land leave the battle they have one against another. [34] And an innumerable multitude shall be gathered together, as thou sawest them, willing to come, and to overcome him by fighting. [35] But he shall stand upon the top of the mount Sion. [36] And Sion shall come, and shall be shewed to all men, being prepared and builded, like as thou sawest the hill graven without hands. [37] And this my Son shall rebuke the wicked inventions of those nations, which for their wicked life are fallen into the tempest; [38] and shall lay before them their evil thoughts, and the torments wherewith they shall begin to be tormented, which are like unto a flame: and he shall destroy them without labour by the law which is like unto me. [39] And whereas thou sawest that he gathered another peaceable multitude unto him; [40] those are the ten tribes, which were carried away prisoners out of their own land in the time of Osea the king, whom Salmanasar the king of Assyria led away captive, and he carried them over the waters, and so came they into another land. [41] But they took this counsel among themselves, that they would leave the multitude of the heathen, and go forth into a further country, where never mankind dwelt, [42] that they might there keep their statutes, which they never kept in their own land. [43] And they entered into Euphrates by the narrow places of the river. [44] For the most High then shewed signs for them, and held still the flood, till they were passed over. [45] For through that country there was a great way to go, namely, of a year and a half: and the same region is called Arsareth. [46] Then dwelt they there until the latter time; and now when they shall begin to come, [47] the Highest shall stay the springs of the stream again, that they may go through: therefore sawest thou the multitude with peace. [48] But those that be left behind of thy people are they that are found within my borders. [49] Now when he destroyeth the multitude of the nations that are gathered together, he shall defend his people that remain. [50] And then shall he shew them great wonders. [51] Then said I, O Lord that bearest rule, shew me this: Wherefore have I seen the man coming up from the midst of the sea? [52] And he said unto me, Like as thou canst neither seek out nor know the things that are in the deep of the sea: even so can no man upon earth see my Son, or those that be with him, but in the day time. [53] This is the interpretation of the dream which thou sawest, and whereby thou only art here lightened. [54] For thou hast forsaken thine own way, and applied thy diligence unto my law, and sought it. [55] Thy life hast thou ordered in wisdom, and hast called understanding thy mother. [56] And therefore have I shewed thee the treasures of the Highest: after other three days I will speak other things unto thee, and declare unto thee mighty and wondrous things. [57] Then went I forth into the field, giving praise and thanks greatly unto the most High because of his wonders which he did in time; [58] and because he governeth the same, and such things as fall in their seasons: and there I sat three days.

14

[1] And it came to pass upon the third day, I sat under an oak, and, behold, there came a voice out of a bush over against me, and said, Esdras, Esdras. [2] And I said, Here am I, Lord. And I stood up upon my feet. [3] Then said he unto me, In the bush I did manifestly reveal myself unto Moses, and talked with him, when my people served in Egypt: [4] And I sent him and led my people out of Egypt, and brought him up to the mount of Sinai, where I held him by me a long season, [5] and told him many wondrous things, and shewed him the

secrets of the times, and the end; and commanded him, saying, [6] These words shalt thou declare, and these shalt thou hide. [7] And now I say unto thee, [8] that thou lay up in thy heart the signs that I have shewed, and the dreams that thou hast seen, and the interpretations which thou hast heard: [9] For thou shalt be taken away from all, and from henceforth thou shalt remain with my Son, and with such as be like thee, until the times be ended. [10] For the world hath lost his youth, and the times begin to wax old. [11] For the world is divided into twelve parts, and the ten parts of it are gone already, and half of a tenth part: [12] And there remaineth that which is after the half of the tenth part. [13] Now therefore set thine house in order, and reprove thy people, comfort such of them as be in trouble, and now renounce corruption, [14] let go from thee mortal thoughts, cast away the burdens of man, put off now the weak nature, [15] and set aside the thoughts that are most heavy unto thee, and haste thee to flee from these times. [16] For yet greater evils than those which thou hast seen happen shall be done hereafter. [17] For look how much the world shall be weaker through age, so much the more shall evils increase upon them that dwell therein. [18] For the time is fled far away, and leasing is hard at hand: for now hasteth the vision to come, which thou hast seen. [19] Then answered I before thee, and said, [20] Behold, Lord, I will go, as thou hast commanded me, and reprove the people which are present: but they that shall be born afterward, who shall admonish them? thus the world is set in darkness, and they that dwell therein are without light. [21] For thy law is burnt, therefore no man knoweth the things that are done of thee, or the work that shall begin. [22] But if I have found grace before thee, send the Holy Ghost into me, and I shall write all that hath been done in the world since the beginning, which were written in thy law, that men may find thy path, and that they which will live in the latter days may live. [23] And he answered me, saying, Go thy way, gather the people together, and say unto them, that they seek thee not for forty days. [24] But look thou prepare thee many box trees, and take with thee Sarea, Dabria, Selemia, Ecanus, and Asiel, these five which are ready to write swiftly; [25] and come hither, and I shall light a candle of understanding in thine heart, which shall not be put out, till the things be performed which thou shalt begin to write. [26] And when thou hast done, some things shalt thou publish, and some things shalt thou shew secretly to the wise: to morrow this hour shalt thou begin to write. [27] Then went I forth, as he commanded, and gathered all the people together, and said, [28] Hear these words, O Israel. [29] Our fathers at the beginning were strangers in Egypt, from whence they were delivered: [30] and received the law of life, which they kept not, which ye also have transgressed after them. [31] Then was the land, even the land of Sion, parted among you by lot: but your fathers, and ye yourselves, have done unrighteousness, and have not kept the ways which the Highest commanded you. [32] And forasmuch as he is a righteous judge, he took from you in time the thing that he had given you. [33] And now are ye here, and your brethren among you. [34] Therefore if so be that ye will subdue your own understanding, and reform your hearts, ye shall be kept alive and after death ye shall obtain mercy. [35] For after death shall the judgment come, when we shall live again: and then shall the names of the righteous be manifest, and the works of the ungodly shall be declared. [36] Let no man therefore come unto me now, nor seek after me these forty days. [37] So I took the five men, as he commanded me, and we went into the field, and remained there. [38] And the next day, behold, a voice called me, saying, Esdras, open thy mouth, and drink that I give thee to drink. [39] Then opened I my mouth, and, behold, he reached me a full cup, which was full as it were with water, but the colour of it was like fire. [40] And I took it, and drank: and when I had drunk of it, my heart uttered understanding, and wisdom grew in my breast, for my spirit strengthened my memory: [41] And my mouth was opened, and shut no more. [42] The Highest gave understanding unto the five men, and they wrote the wonderful visions of the night that were told, which they knew not: and they sat forty days, and they wrote in the day, and at night they ate bread. [43] As for me. I spake in the day, and I held not my tongue by night. [44] In forty days they wrote two hundred and four books. [45] And it came to pass, when the forty days were filled, that the Highest spake, saying, The first that thou hast written publish openly, that the worthy and unworthy may read it: [46] But keep the seventy last, that thou mayest deliver them only to such as be wise among the people: [47] For in them is the spring of understanding, the fountain of wisdom, and the stream of knowledge. [48] And I did so.

15 [1] Behold, speak thou in the ears of my people the words of prophecy, which I will put in thy mouth, saith the Lord: [2] And cause them to be written in paper: for they are faithful and true. [3] Fear not the imaginations against thee, let not the incredulity of them trouble thee, that speak against thee. [4] For all the unfaithful shall die in their unfaithfulness. [5] Behold, saith the Lord, I will bring plagues upon the world; the sword,

famine, death, and destruction. [6] For wickedness hath exceedingly polluted the whole earth, and their hurtful works are fulfilled. [7] Therefore saith the Lord, [8] I will hold my tongue no more as touching their wickedness, which they profanely commit, neither will I suffer them in those things, in which they wickedly exercise themselves: behold, the innocent and righteous blood crieth unto me, and the souls of the just complain continually. [9] And therefore, saith the Lord, I will surely avenge them, and receive unto me all the innocent blood from among them. [10] Behold, my people is led as a flock to the slaughter: I will not suffer them now to dwell in the land of Egypt: [11] But I will bring them with a mighty hand and a stretched out arm, and smite Egypt with plagues, as before, and will destroy all the land thereof. [12] Egypt shall mourn, and the foundation of it shall be smitten with the plague and punishment that God shall bring upon it. [13] They that till the ground shall mourn: for their seeds shall fail through the blasting and hail, and with a fearful constellation. [14] Woe to the world and them that dwell therein! [15] For the sword and their destruction draweth nigh, and one people shall stand up and fight against another, and swords in their hands. [16] For there shall be sedition among men, and invading one another; they shall not regard their kings nor princes, and the course of their actions shall stand in their power. [17] A man shall desire to go into a city, and shall not be able. [18] For because of their pride the cities shall be troubled, the houses shall be destroyed, and men shall be afraid. [19] A man shall have no pity upon his neighbour, but shall destroy their houses with the sword, and spoil their goods, because of the lack of bread, and for great tribulation. [20] Behold, saith God, I will call together all the kings of the earth to reverence me, which are from the rising of the sun, from the south, from the east, and Libanus; to turn themselves one against another, and repay the things that they have done to them. [21] Like as they do yet this day unto my chosen, so will I do also, and recompense in their bosom. Thus saith the Lord God; [22] My right hand shall not spare the sinners, and my sword shall not cease over them that shed innocent blood upon the earth. [23] The fire is gone forth from his wrath, and hath consumed the foundations of the earth, and the sinners, like the straw that is kindled. [24] Woe to them that sin, and keep not my commandments! saith the Lord. [25] I will not spare them: go your way, ye children, from the power, defile not my sanctuary. [26] For the Lord knoweth all them that sin against him, and therefore delivereth he them unto death and destruction. [27] For now are the plagues come upon the whole earth and ye shall remain in them: for God shall not deliver you, because ye have sinned against him. [28] Behold an horrible vision, and the appearance thereof from the east: [29] where the nations of the dragons of Arabia shall come out with many chariots, and the multitude of them shall be carried as the wind upon earth, that all they which hear them may fear and tremble. [30] Also the Carmanians raging in wrath shall go forth as the wild boars of the wood, and with great power shall they come, and join battle with them, and shall waste a portion of the land of the Assyrians. [31] And then shall the dragons have the upper hand, remembering their nature; and if they shall turn themselves, conspiring together in great power to persecute them, [32] then these shall be troubled, and keep silence through their power, and shall flee. [33] And from the land of the Assyrians shall the enemy besiege them, and consume some of them, and in their host shall be fear and dread, and strife among their kings. [34] Behold clouds from the east and from the north unto the south, and they are very horrible to look upon, full of wrath and storm. [35] They shall smite one upon another, and they shall smite down a great multitude of stars upon the earth, even their own star; and blood shall be from the sword unto the belly, [36] and dung of men unto the camel's hough. [37] And there shall be great fearfulness and trembling upon earth: and they that see the wrath shall be afraid, and trembling shall come upon them. [38] And then shall there come great storms from the south, and from the north, and another part from the west. [39] And strong winds shall arise from the east, and shall open it; and the cloud which he raised up in wrath, and the star stirred to cause fear toward the east and west wind, shall be destroyed. [40] The great and mighty clouds shall be puffed up full of wrath, and the star, that they may make all the earth afraid, and them that dwell therein; and they shall pour out over every high and eminent place an horrible star, [41] fire, and hail, and flying swords, and many waters, that all fields may be full, and all rivers, with the abundance of great waters. [42] And they shall break down the cities and walls, mountains and hills, trees of the wood, and grass of the meadows, and their corn. [43] And they shall go steadfastly unto Babylon, and make her afraid. [44] They shall come to her, and besiege her, the star and all wrath shall they pour out upon her: then shall the dust and smoke go up unto the heaven, and all they that be about her shall bewail her. [45] And they that remain under her shall do service unto them that have put her in fear. [46] And thou, Asia, that art partaker of the hope of Babylon, and art the glory of her person: [47] Woe be unto thee, thou wretch, because thou hast made thyself like unto her; and hast decked thy daughters in whoredom, that they might please and glory in thy lovers, which have always desired to commit whoredom with thee. [48] Thou hast followed her that is hated in all her works and inventions: therefore saith God, [49] I will send plagues upon thee; widowhood, poverty, famine, sword, and pestilence, to waste thy houses with destruction and death. [50] And the glory of thy Power shall be dried up as a flower, when the heat shall arise that is sent over thee. [51] Thou shalt be weakened as a poor woman with stripes, and as one chastised with wounds, so that the mighty and lovers shall not be able to receive thee. [52] Would I with jealousy have so proceeded against thee, saith the Lord, [53] if thou hadst not always slain my chosen, exalting the stroke of thine hands, and saying over their dead, when thou wast drunken, [54] set forth the beauty of thy countenance? [55] The reward of thy whoredom shall be in thy bosom, therefore shalt thou receive recompence. [56] Like as thou hast done unto my chosen, saith the Lord, even so shall God do unto thee, and shall deliver thee into mischief. [57] Thy children shall die of hunger, and thou shalt fall through the sword: thy cities shall be broken down, and all thine shall perish with the sword in the field. [58] They that be in the mountains shall die of hunger, and eat their own flesh, and drink their own blood, for very hunger of bread, and thirst of water. [59] Thou as unhappy shalt come through the sea, and receive plagues again. [60] And in the passage they shall rush on the idle city, and shall destroy some portion of thy land, and consume part of thy glory, and shall return to Babylon that was destroyed. [61] And thou shalt be cast down by them as stubble, and they shall be unto thee as fire; [62] and shall consume thee, and thy cities, thy land, and thy mountains; all thy woods and thy fruitful trees shall they burn up with fire. [63] Thy children shall they carry away captive, and, look, what thou hast, they shall spoil it, and mar the beauty of thy face.

16 [1] Woe be unto thee, Babylon, and Asia! woe be unto thee, Egypt and Syria! [2] Gird up yourselves with cloths of sack and hair, bewail your children, and be sorry; for your destruction is at hand. [3] A sword is sent upon you, and who may turn it back? [4] A fire is sent among you, and who may quench it? [5] Plagues are sent unto you, and what is he that may drive them away? [6] May any man drive away an hungry lion in the wood? or may any one quench the fire in stubble, when it hath begun to burn? [7] May one turn again the arrow that is shot of a strong archer? [8] The mighty Lord sendeth the plagues and who is he that can drive them away? [9] A fire shall go forth from his wrath, and who is he that may quench it? [10] He shall cast lightnings, and who shall not fear? he shall thunder, and who shall not be afraid? [11] The Lord shall threaten, and who shall not be utterly beaten to powder at his presence? [12] The earth quaketh, and the foundations thereof; the sea ariseth up with waves from the deep, and the waves of it are troubled, and the fishes thereof also, before the Lord, and before the glory of his power: [13] For strong is his right hand that bendeth the bow, his arrows that he shooteth are sharp, and shall not miss, when they begin to be shot into the ends of the world. [14] Behold, the plagues are sent, and shall not return again, until they come upon the earth. [15] The fire is kindled, and shall not be put out, till it consume the foundation of the earth. [16] Like as an arrow which is shot of a mighty

archer returneth not backward: even so the plagues that shall be sent upon earth shall not return again. [17] Woe is me! woe is me! who will deliver me in those days? [18] The beginning of sorrows and great mournings; the beginning of famine and great dearth; the beginning of wars, and the powers shall stand in fear; the beginning of evils! what shall I do when these evils shall come? [19] Behold, famine and plague, tribulation and anguish, are sent as scourges for amendment. [20] But for all these things they shall not turn from their wickedness, nor be always mindful of the scourges. [21] Behold, victuals shall be so good, cheap upon earth, that they shall think themselves to be in good case, and even then shall evils grow upon earth, sword, famine, and great confusion. [22] For many of them that dwell upon earth shall perish of famine; and the others, that escape the hunger, shall the sword destroy. [23] And the dead shall be cast out as dung, and there shall be no man to comfort them: for the earth shall be wasted, and the cities shall be cast down. [24] There shall be no man left to till the earth, and to sow it. [25] The trees shall give fruit, and who shall gather them? [26] The grapes shall ripen, and who shall tread them? for all places shall be desolate of men: [27] so that one man shall desire to see another, and to hear his voice. [28] For of a city there shall be ten left, and two of the field, which shall hide themselves in the thick groves, and in the clefts of the rocks. [29] As in an orchard of olives upon every tree there are left three or four olives; [30] or as when a vineyard is gathered, there are left some clusters of them that diligently seek through the vineyard: [31] even so in those days there shall be three or four left by them that search their houses with the sword. [32] And the earth shall be laid waste, and the fields thereof shall wax old, and her ways and all her paths shall grow full of thorns, because no man shall travel therethrough. [33] The virgins shall mourn, having no bridegrooms; the women shall mourn, having no husbands; their daughters shall mourn, having no helpers. [34] In the wars shall their bridegrooms be destroyed, and their husbands shall perish of famine. [35] Hear now these things and understand them, ye servants of the Lord. [36] Behold, the word of the Lord, receive it: believe not the gods of whom the Lord spake. [37] Behold, the plagues draw nigh, and are not slack. [38] As when a woman with child in the ninth month bringeth forth her son, with two or three hours of her birth great pains compass her womb, which pains, when the child cometh forth, they slack not a moment: [39] Even so shall not the plagues be slack to come upon the earth, and the world shall mourn, and sorrows shall come upon it on every side. [40] O my people, hear my word: make you ready to thy battle, and in those evils be even as pilgrims upon the earth. [41] He that selleth, let him be as he that fleeth away: and he that buyeth, as one that will lose: [42] He that occupieth merchandise, as he that hath no profit by it: and he that buildeth, as he that shall not dwell therein: [43] He that soweth, as if he should not reap: so also he that planteth the vineyard, as he that shall not gather the grapes: [44] They that marry, as they that shall get no children; and they that marry not, as the widowers. [45] And therefore they that labour, labour in vain: [46] For strangers shall reap their fruits, and spoil their goods, overthrow their houses, and take their children captives, for in captivity and famine shall they get children. [47] And they that occupy their merchandise with robbery, the more they deck their cities, their houses, their possessions, and their own persons: [48] the more will I be angry with them for their sin, saith the Lord. [49] Like as a whore envieth a right honest and virtuous woman: [50] so shall righteousness hate iniquity, when she decketh herself, and shall accuse her to her face, when he cometh that shall defend him that diligently searcheth out every sin upon earth. [51] And therefore be ye not like thereunto, nor to the works thereof. [52] For yet a little, and iniquity shall be taken away out of the earth, and righteousness shall reign among you. [53] Let not the sinner say that he hath not sinned: for God shall burn coals of fire upon his head, which saith before the Lord God and his glory, I have not sinned. [54] Behold, the Lord knoweth all the works of men, their imaginations, their thoughts, and their hearts: [55] which spake but the word, Let the earth be made; and it was made: Let the heaven be made; and it was created. [56] In his word were the stars made, and he knoweth the number of them. [57] He searcheth the deep, and the treasures thereof; he hath measured the sea, and what it containeth. [58] He hath shut the sea in the midst of the waters, and with his word hath he hanged the earth upon the waters. [59] He spreadeth out the heavens like a vault; upon the waters hath he founded it. [60] In the desert hath he made springs of water, and pools upon the tops of the mountains, that the floods might pour down from the high rocks to water the earth. [61] He made man, and put his heart in the midst of the body, and gave him breath, life, and understanding. [62] Yea and the Spirit of Almighty God, which made all things, and searcheth out all hidden things in the secrets of the earth, [63] surely he knoweth your inventions, and what ye think in your hearts, even them that sin, and would hide their sin. [64] Therefore hath the Lord exactly searched out all your works, and he will put you all to shame. [65] And when your sins are brought forth, ye shall be ashamed before men, and your own sins shall be your accusers in that day. [66] What will ye do? or how will ye hide your sins before God and his angels? [67] Behold, God himself is the judge, fear him: leave off from your sins, and forget your iniquities, to meddle no more with them for ever: so shall God lead you forth, and deliver you from all trouble. [68] For, behold, the burning wrath of a great multitude is kindled over you, and they shall take away certain of you, and feed you, being idle, with things offered unto idols. [69] And they that consent unto them shall be had in derision and in reproach, and trodden under foot. [70] For there shall be in every place, and in the next cities, a great insurrection upon those that fear the Lord. [71] They shall be like mad men, sparing none, but still spoiling and destroying those that fear the Lord. [72] For they shall waste and take away their goods, and cast them out of their houses. [73] Then shall they be known, who are my chosen; and they shall be tried as the gold in the fire. [74] Hear, O ye my beloved, saith the Lord: behold, the days of trouble are at hand, but I will deliver you from the same. [75] Be ye not afraid neither doubt; for God is your guide, [76] and the guide of them who keep my commandments and precepts, saith the Lord God: let not your sins weigh you down, and let not your iniquities lift up themselves. [77] Woe be unto them that are bound with their sins, and covered with their iniquities like as a field is covered over with bushes, and the path thereof covered with thorns, that no man may travel through! [78] It is left undressed, and is cast into the fire to be consumed therewith.

THE BOOK OF TOBIT

1 [1] The book of the words of Tobit, son of Tobiel, the son of Ananiel, the son of Aduel, the son of Gabael, of the seed of Asael, of the tribe of Nephthali; [2] who in the time of Enemessar king of the Assyrians was led captive out of Thisbe, which is at the right hand of that city, which is called properly Nephthali in Galilee above Aser. [3] I Tobit have walked all the days of my life in the ways of truth and justice, and I did many almsdeeds to my brethren, and my nation, who came with me to Nineve, into the land of the Assyrians. [4] And when I was in mine own country, in the land of Israel, being but young, all the tribe of Nephthali my father fell from the house of Jerusalem, which was chosen out of all the tribes of Israel, that all the tribes should sacrifice there, where the temple of the habitation of the most High was consecrated and built for all ages. [5] Now all the tribes which together revolted, and the house of my father Nephthali, sacrificed unto the heifer Baal. [6] But I alone went often to Jerusalem at the feasts, as it was ordained unto all the people of Israel by an everlasting decree, having the firstfruits and tenths of increase,

with that which was first shorn; and them gave I at the altar to the priests the children of Aaron. [7] The first tenth part of all increase I gave to the sons of Aaron, who ministered at Jerusalem: another tenth part I sold away, and went, and spent it every year at Jerusalem: [8] and the third I gave unto them to whom it was meet, as Debora my father's mother had commanded me, because I was left an orphan by my father. [9] Furthermore, when I was come to the age of a man, I married Anna of mine own kindred, and of her I begat Tobias. [10] And when we were carried away captives to Nineve, all my brethren and those that were of my kindred did eat of the bread of the Gentiles. [11] But I kept myself from eating; [12] because I remembered God with all my heart. [13] And the most High gave me grace and favour before Enemessar, so that I was his purveyor. [14] And I went into Media, and left in trust with Gabael, the brother of Gabrias, at Rages, a city of Media, ten talents of silver. [15] Now when Enemessar was dead, Sennacherib his son reigned in his stead; whose estate was troubled, that I could not go into Media. [16] And in the time of Enemessar I gave many alms to my brethren, and gave my bread to the hungry, [17] and my clothes to the naked: and if I saw any of my nation dead, or cast about the walls of Nineve, I buried him. [18] And if the king Sennacherib had slain any, when he was come, and fled from Judea, I buried them privily; for in his wrath he killed many; but the bodies were not found, when they were sought for of the king. [19] And when one of the Ninevites went and complained of me to the king, that I buried them, and hid myself; understanding that I was sought for to be put to death, I withdrew myself for fear. [20] Then all my goods were forcibly taken away, neither was there any thing left me, besides my wife Anna and my son Tobias. [21] And there passed not five and fifty days, before two of his sons killed him, and they fled into the mountains of Ararath; and Sarchedonus his son reigned in his stead; who appointed over his father's accounts, and over all his affairs, Achiacharus, my brother Anael's son. [22] And Achiacharus intreating for me, I returned to Nineve. Now Achiacharus was cupbearer, and keeper of the signet, and steward, and overseer of the accounts: and Sarchedonus appointed him next unto him: and he was my brother's son.

2 [1] Now when I was come home again, and my wife Anna was restored unto me, with my son Tobias, in the feast of Pentecost, which is the holy feast of the seven weeks, there was a good dinner prepared me, in the which I sat down to eat. [2] And when I saw abundance of meat, I said to my son, Go and bring what poor man soever thou shalt find out of our brethren, who is mindful of the Lord; and, lo, I tarry for thee. [3] But he came again, and said, Father, one of our nation is strangled, and is cast out in the marketplace. [4] Then before I had tasted of any meat, I started up, and took him up into a room until the going down of the sun. [5] Then I returned, and washed myself, and ate my meat in heaviness, [6] remembering that prophecy of Amos, as he said, Your feasts shall be turned into mourning, and all your mirth into lamentation. [7] Therefore I wept: and after the going down of the sun I went and made a grave, and buried him. [8] But my neighbours mocked me, and said, This man is not yet afraid to be put to death for this matter: who fled away; and yet, lo, he burieth the dead again. [9] The same night also I returned from the burial, and slept by the wall of my courtyard, being pol-

luted, and my face was uncovered: [10] And I knew not that there were sparrows in the wall, and mine eyes being open, the sparrows muted warm dung into mine eyes, and a whiteness came in mine eyes: and I went to the physicians, but they helped me not: moreover Achiacharus did nourish me, until I went into Elymais. [11] And my wife Anna did take women's works to do. [12] And when she had sent them home to the owners, they paid her wages, and gave her also besides a kid. [13] And when it was in my house, and began to cry, I said unto her, From whence is this kid? is it not stolen? render it to the owners; for it is not lawful to eat any thing that is stolen. [14] But she replied upon me, It was given for a gift more than the wages. Howbeit I did not believe her, but bade her render it to the owners: and I was abashed at her. But she replied upon me, Where are thine alms and thy righteous deeds? behold, thou and all thy works are known.

3 [1] Then I being grieved did weep, and in my sorrow prayed, saying, [2] O Lord, thou art just, and all thy works and all thy ways are mercy and truth, and thou judgest truly and justly for ever. [3] Remember me, and look on me, punish me not for my sins and ignorances, and the sins of my fathers, who have sinned before thee: [4] For they obeyed not thy commandments: wherefore thou hast delivered us for a spoil, and unto captivity, and unto death, and for a proverb of reproach to all the nations among whom we are dispersed. [5] And now thy judgments are many and true: deal with me according to my sins and my fathers': because we have not kept thy commandments, neither have walked in truth before thee. [6] Now therefore deal with me as seemeth best unto thee, and command my spirit to be taken

from me, that I may be dissolved, and become earth: for it is profitable for me to die rather than to live, because I have heard false reproaches, and have much sorrow: command therefore that I may now be delivered out of this distress, and go into the everlasting place: turn not thy face away from me. [7] It came to pass the same day, that in Ecbatane, a city of Media, Sara the daughter of Raguel was also reproached by her father's maids; [8] because that she had been married to seven husbands, whom Asmodeus the evil spirit had killed, before they had lain with her. Dost thou not know, said they, that thou hast strangled thine husbands? thou hast had already seven husbands, neither wast thou named after any of them. [9] Wherefore dost thou beat us for them? if they be dead, go thy ways after them, let us never see of thee either son or daughter. [10] When she heard these things, she was very sorrowful, so that she thought to have strangled herself; and she said, I am the only daughter of my father, and if I do this, it shall be a reproach unto him, and I shall bring his old age with sorrow unto the grave. [11] Then she prayed toward the window, and said, Blessed art thou, O Lord my God, and thine holy and glorious name is blessed and honourable for ever: let all thy works praise thee for ever. [12] And now, O Lord, I set mine eyes and my face toward thee, [13] and say, Take me out of the earth, that I may hear no more the reproach. [14] Thou knowest, Lord, that I am pure from all sin with man, [15] and that I never polluted my name, nor the name of my father, in the land of my captivity: I am the only daughter of my father, neither hath he any child to be his heir, neither any near kinsman, nor any son of his alive, to whom I may keep myself for a wife: my seven husbands are already dead; and why should I live? but if it please not thee that I should die, command some regard to be had of me, and pity taken of me, that I hear no more reproach. [16] So the prayers of them both were heard before the majesty of the great God. [17] And Raphael was sent to heal them both, that is, to scale away the whiteness of Tobit's eyes, and to give Sara the daughter of Raguel for a wife to Tobias the son of Tobit; and to bind Asmodeus the evil spirit; because she belonged to Tobias by right of inheritance. The selfsame time came Tobit home, and entered into his house, and Sara the daughter of Raguel came down from her upper chamber.

4 [1] In that day Tobit remembered the money which he had committed to Gabael in Rages of Media, [2] and said within himself, I have wished for death; wherefore do I not call for my son Tobias that I may signify to him of the money before I die? [3] And when he had called him, he said, My son, when I am dead, bury me; and despise not thy mother, but honour her all the days of thy life, and do that which shall please her, and grieve her not. [4] Remember, my son, that she saw many dangers for thee, when thou wast in her womb: and when she is dead, bury her by me in one grave. [5] My son, be mindful of the Lord our God all thy days, and let not thy will be set to sin, or to transgress his commandments: do uprightly all thy life long, and follow not the ways of unrighteousness. [6] For if thou deal truly, thy doings shall prosperously succeed to thee, and to all them that live justly. [7] Give alms of thy substance; and when thou givest alms, let not thine eye be envious, neither turn thy face from any poor, and the face of God shall not be turned away from thee. [8] If thou hast abundance give alms accordingly: if thou have but a little, be not afraid to give according to that little: [9] For thou layest

up a good treasure for thyself against the day of necessity. [10] Because that alms do deliver from death, and suffereth not to come into darkness. [11] For alms is a good gift unto all that give it in the sight of the most High. [12] Beware of all whoredom, my son, and chiefly take a wife of the seed of thy fathers, and take not a strange woman to wife, which is not of thy father's tribe: for we are the children of the prophets, Noe, Abraham, Isaac, and Jacob: remember, my son, that our fathers from the beginning, even that they all married wives of their own kindred, and were blessed in their children, and their seed shall inherit the land. [13] Now therefore, my son, love thy brethren, and despise not in thy heart thy brethren, the sons and daughters of thy people, in not taking a wife of them: for in pride is destruction and much trouble, and in lewdness is decay and great want: for lewdness is the mother of famine. [14] Let not the wages of any man, which hath wrought for thee, tarry with thee, but give him it out of hand: for if thou serve God, he will also repay thee: be circumspect my son, in all things thou doest, and be wise in all thy conversation. [15] Do that to no man which thou hatest: drink not wine to make thee drunken: neither let drunkenness go with thee in thy journey. [16] Give of thy bread to the hungry, and of thy garments to them that are naked; and according to thine abundance give alms: and let not thine eye be envious, when thou givest alms. [17] Pour out thy bread on the burial of the just, but give nothing to the wicked. [18] Ask counsel of all that are wise, and despise not any counsel that is profitable. [19] Bless the Lord thy God always, and desire of him that thy ways may be directed, and that all thy paths and counsels may prosper: for every nation hath not counsel; but the Lord himself giveth all good things, and he humbleth whom he will, as he will; now therefore, my son, remember my commandments, neither let them be put out of thy mind. [20] And now I signify this to thee, that I committed ten talents to Gabael the son of Gabrias at Rages in Media. [21] And fear not, my son, that we are made poor: for thou hast much wealth, if thou fear God, and depart from all sin, and do that which is pleasing in his sight.

5 [1] Tobias then answered and said, Father, I will do all things which thou hast commanded me: [2] But how can I receive the money, seeing I know him not? [3] Then he gave him the handwriting, and said unto him, Seek thee a man which may go with thee, while I yet live, and I will give him wages: and go and receive the money. [4] Therefore when he went to seek a man, he found Raphael that was an angel. [5] But he knew not; and he said unto him, Canst thou go with me to Rages? and knowest thou those places well? [6] To whom the angel said, I will go with thee, and I know the way well: for I have lodged with our brother Gabael. [7] Then Tobias said unto him, Tarry for me, till I tell my father. [8] Then he said unto him, Go and tarry not. So he went in and said to his father, Behold, I have found one which will go with me. Then he said, Call him unto me, that I may know of what tribe he is, and whether he be a trusty man to go with thee. [9] So he called him, and he came in, and they saluted one another. [10] Then Tobit said unto him, Brother, shew me of what tribe and family thou art. [11] To whom he said, Dost thou seek for a tribe or family, or an hired man to go with thy son? Then Tobit said unto him, I would know, brother, thy kindred and name. [12] Then he said, I am Azarias, the son of Ananias the great, and of thy brethren. [13] Then

Tobit said, Thou art welcome, brother; be not now angry with me, because I have enquired to know thy tribe and thy family; for thou art my brother, of an honest and good stock: for I know Ananias and Jonathas, sons of that great Samaias, as we went together to Jerusalem to worship, and offered the firstborn, and the tenths of the fruits; and they were not seduced with the error of our brethren: my brother, thou art of a good stock. [14] But tell me, what wages shall I give thee? wilt thou a drachm a day, and things necessary, as to mine own son? [15] Yea, moreover, if ye return safe, I will add something to thy wages. [16] So they were well pleased. Then said he to Tobias, Prepare thyself for the journey, and God send you a good journey. And when his son had prepared all things for the journey, his father said, Go thou with this man, and God, which dwelleth in heaven, prosper your journey, and the angel of God keep you company. So they went forth both, and the young man's dog with them. [17] But Anna his mother wept, and said to Tobit, Why hast thou sent away our son? is he not the staff of our hand, in going in and out before us? [18] Be not greedy to add money to money: but let it be as refuse in respect of our child. [19] For that which the Lord hath given us to live with doth suffice us. [20] Then said Tobit to her, Take no care, my sister; he shall return in safety, and thine eyes shall see him. [21] For the good angel will keep him company, and his journey shall be prosperous, and he shall return safe. [22] Then she made an end of weeping.

6 [1] And as they went on their journey, they came in the evening to the river Tigris, and they lodged there. [2] And when the young man went down to wash himself, a fish leaped out of the river, and would have

devoured him. [3] Then the angel said unto him, Take the fish. And the young man laid hold of the fish, and drew it to land. [4] To whom the angel said, Open the fish, and take the heart and the liver and the gall, and put them up safely. [5] So the young man did as the angel commanded him; and when they had roasted the fish, they did eat it: then they both went on their way, till they drew near to Ecbatane. [6] Then the young man said to the angel, Brother Azarias, to what use is the heart and the liver and the gall of the fish? [7] And he said unto him, Touching the heart and the liver, if a devil or an evil spirit trouble any, we must make a smoke thereof before the man or the woman, and the party shall be no more vexed. [8] As for the gall, it is good to anoint a man that hath whiteness in his eyes, and he shall be healed. [9] And when they were come near to Rages, [10] the angel said to the young man, Brother, to day we shall lodge with Raguel, who is thy cousin; he also hath one only daughter, named Sara; I will speak for her, that she may be given thee for a wife. [11] For to thee doth the right of her appertain, seeing thou only art of her kindred. [12] And the maid is fair and wise: now therefore hear me, and I will speak to her father; and when we return from Rages we will celebrate the marriage: for I know that Raguel cannot marry her to another according to the law of Moses, but he shall be guilty of death, because the right of inheritance doth rather appertain to thee than to any other. [13] Then the young man answered the angel, I have heard, brother Azarias that this maid hath been given to seven men, who all died in the marriage chamber. [14] And now I am the only son of my father, and I am afraid, lest if I go in unto her, I die, as the other before: for a wicked spirit loveth her, which hurteth no body, but those which come unto her; wherefore I also fear lest I die, and bring my father's and my mother's life because of me to the grave with sorrow: for they have no other son to bury them. [15] Then the angel said unto him, Dost thou not remember the precepts which thy father gave thee, that thou shouldest marry a wife of thine own kindred? wherefore hear me, O my brother; for she shall be given thee to wife; and make thou no reckoning of the evil spirit; for this same night shall she be given thee in marriage. [16] And when thou shalt come into the marriage chamber, thou shalt take the ashes of perfume, and shalt lay upon them some of the heart and liver of the fish, and shalt make a smoke with it: [17] And the devil shall smell it, and flee away, and never come again any more: but when thou shalt come to her, rise up both of you, and pray to God which is merciful, who will have pity on you, and save you: fear not, for she is appointed unto thee from the beginning; and thou shalt preserve her, and she shall go with thee. Moreover I suppose that she shall bear thee children. Now when Tobias had heard these things, he loved her, and his heart was effectually joined to her.

7 [1] And when they were come to Ecbatane, they came to the house of Raguel, and Sara met them: and after they had saluted one another, she brought them into the house. [2] Then said Raguel to Edna his wife, How like is this young man to Tobit my cousin! [3] And Raguel asked them, From whence are ye, brethren? To whom they said, We are of the sons of Nephthali, which are captives in Nineve. [4] Then he said to them, Do ye know Tobit our kinsman? And they said, We know him. Then said he, Is he in good health? [5] And they said, He is both alive, and in good health: and Tobias

said, He is my father. [6] Then Raguel leaped up, and kissed him, and wept, [7] and blessed him, and said unto him, Thou art the son of an honest and good man. But when he had heard that Tobit was blind, he was sorrowful, and wept. [8] And likewise Edna his wife and Sara his daughter wept. Moreover they entertained them cheerfully; and after that they had killed a ram of the flock, they set store of meat on the table. Then said Tobias to Raphael, Brother Azarias, speak of those things of which thou didst talk in the way, and let this business be dispatched. [9] So he communicated the matter with Raguel: and Raguel said to Tobias, Eat and drink, and make merry: [10] For it is meet that thou shouldest marry my daughter: nevertheless I will declare unto thee the truth. [11] I have given my daughter in marriage to seven men, who died that night they came in unto her: nevertheless for the present be merry. But Tobias said, I will eat nothing here, till we agree and swear one to another. [12] Raguel said, Then take her from henceforth according to the manner, for thou art her cousin, and she is thine, and the merciful God give you good success in all things. [13] Then he called his daughter Sara, and she came to her father, and he took her by the hand, and gave her to be wife to Tobias, saying, Behold, take her after the law of Moses, and lead her away to thy father. And he blessed them; [14] and called Edna his wife, and took paper, and did write an instrument of covenants, and sealed it. [15] Then they began to eat. [16] After Raguel called his wife Edna, and said unto her, Sister, prepare another chamber, and bring her in thither. [17] Which when she had done as he had bidden her, she brought her thither: and she wept, and she received the tears of her daughter, and said unto her, [18] Be of good comfort, my daughter; the Lord of heaven and earth give thee joy for this thy sorrow: be of good comfort, my daughter.

8 [1] And when they had supped, they brought Tobias in unto her. [2] And as he went, he remembered the words of Raphael, and took the ashes of the perfumes, and put the heart and the liver of the fish thereupon, and made a smoke therewith. [3] The which smell when the evil spirit had smelled, he fled into the utmost parts of Egypt, and the angel bound him. [4] And after that they were both shut in together, Tobias rose out of the bed, and said, Sister, arise, and let us pray that God would have pity on us. [5] Then began Tobias to say, Blessed art thou, O God of our fathers, and blessed is thy holy and glorious name for ever; let the heavens bless thee, and all thy creatures. [6] Thou madest Adam, and gavest him Eve his wife for an helper and stay: of them came mankind: thou hast said, It is not good that man should be alone; let us make unto him an aid like unto himself. [7] And now, O Lord, I take not this my sister for lust but uprightly: therefore mercifully ordain that we may become aged together. [8] And she said with him, Amen. [9] So they slept both that night. And Raguel arose, and went and made a grave, [10] saying, I fear lest he also be dead. [11] But when Raguel was come into his house, [12] he said unto his wife Edna, Send one of the maids, and let her see whether he be alive: if he be not, that we may bury him, and no man know it. [13] So the maid opened the door, and went in, and found them both asleep, [14] and came forth, and told them that he was alive. [15] Then Raguel praised God, and said, O God, thou art worthy to be praised with all pure and holy praise; therefore let thy saints praise thee with all thy creatures; and let all thine angels and thine elect praise

thee for ever. [16] Thou art to be praised, for thou hast made me joyful; and that is not come to me which I suspected; but thou hast dealt with us according to thy great mercy. [17] Thou art to be praised because thou hast had mercy of two that were the only begotten children of their fathers: grant them mercy, O Lord, and finish their life in health with joy and mercy. [18] Then Raguel bade his servants to fill the grave. [19] And he kept the wedding feast fourteen days. [20] For before the days of the marriage were finished, Raguel had said unto him by an oath, that he should not depart till the fourteen days of the marriage were expired; [21] And then he should take the half of his goods, and go in safety to his father; and should have the rest when I and my wife be dead.

9 [1] Then Tobias called Raphael, and said unto him, [2] Brother Azarias, take with thee a servant, and two camels, and go to Rages of Media to Gabael, and bring me the money, and bring him to the wedding. [3] For Raguel hath sworn that I shall not depart. [4] But my father counteth the days; and if I tarry long, he will be very sorry. [5] So Raphael went out, and lodged with Gabael, and gave him the handwriting: who brought forth bags which were sealed up, and gave them to him. [6] And early in the morning they went forth both together, and came to the wedding: and Tobias blessed his wife.

10 [1] Now Tobit his father counted every day: and when the days of the journey were expired, and they came not, [2] then Tobit said, Are they detained? or is Gabael dead, and there is no man to give him the money? [3] Therefore he was very sorry. [4] Then his wife said unto

him, My son is dead, seeing he stayeth long; and she began to bewail him, and said, [5] Now I care for nothing, my son, since I have let thee go, the light of mine eyes. [6] To whom Tobit said, Hold thy peace, take no care, for he is safe. [7] But she said, Hold thy peace, and deceive me not; my son is dead. And she went out every day into the way in which they went, and did eat no meat on the daytime, and ceased not whole nights to bewail her son Tobias, until the fourteen days of the wedding were expired, which Raguel had sworn that he should spend there. Then Tobias said to Raguel, Let me go, for my father and my mother look no more to see me. [8] But his father in law said unto him, Tarry with me, and I will send to thy father, and they shall declare unto him how things go with thee. [9] But Tobias said, No; but let me go to my father. [10] Then Raguel arose, and gave him Sara his wife, and half his goods, servants, and cattle, and money: [11] And he blessed them, and sent them away, saying, The God of heaven give you a prosperous journey, my children. [12] And he said to his daughter, Honour thy father and thy mother in law, which are now thy parents, that I may hear good report of thee. And he kissed her. Edna also said to Tobias, The Lord of heaven restore thee, my dear brother, and grant that I may see thy children of my daughter Sara before I die, that I may rejoice before the Lord: behold, I commit my daughter unto thee of special trust; wherefore do not entreat her evil.

11

[1] After these things Tobias went his way, praising God that he had given him a prosperous journey, and blessed Raguel and Edna his wife, and went on his way till they drew near unto Nineve. [2] Then Raphael said to Tobias, Thou knowest, brother, how thou didst leave

thy father: [3] Let us haste before thy wife, and prepare the house. [4] And take in thine hand the gall of the fish. So they went their way, and the dog went after them. [5] Now Anna sat looking about toward the way for her son. [6] And when she espied him coming, she said to his father, Behold, thy son cometh, and the man that went with him. [7] Then said Raphael, I know, Tobias, that thy father will open his eyes. [8] Therefore anoint thou his eyes with the gall, and being pricked therewith, he shall rub, and the whiteness shall fall away, and he shall see thee. [9] Then Anna ran forth, and fell upon the neck of her son, and said unto him, Seeing I have seen thee, my son, from henceforth I am content to die. And they wept both. [10] Tobit also went forth toward the door, and stumbled: but his son ran unto him, [11] and took hold of his father: and he strake of the gall on his father's eyes, saying, Be of good hope, my father. [12] And when his eyes began to smart, he rubbed them; [13] and the whiteness pilled away from the corners of his eyes: and when he saw his son, he fell upon his neck. [14] And he wept, and said, Blessed art thou, O God, and blessed is thy name for ever; and blessed are all thine holy angels: [15] For thou hast scourged, and hast taken pity on me: for, behold, I see my son Tobias. And his son went in rejoicing, and told his father the great things that had happened to him in Media. [16] Then Tobit went out to meet his daughter in law at the gate of Nineve, rejoicing and praising God: and they which saw him go marvelled, because he had received his sight. [17] But Tobit gave thanks before them, because God had mercy on him. And when he came near to Sara his daughter in law, he blessed her, saying, Thou art welcome, daughter: God be blessed, which hath brought thee unto us, and blessed be thy father and thy mother. And there was joy among all his brethren which were at Nineve. [18] And Achiacharus, and Nasbas his brother's son, came: [19] And Tobias' wedding was kept seven days with great joy.

12 [1] Then Tobit called his son Tobias, and said unto him, My son, see that the man have his wages, which went with thee, and thou must give him more. [2] And Tobias said unto him, O father, it is no harm to me to give him half of those things which I have brought: [3] For he hath brought me again to thee in safety, and made whole my wife, and brought me the money, and likewise healed thee. [4] Then the old man said, It is due unto him. [5] So he called the angel, and he said unto him, Take half of all that ye have brought and go away in safety. [6] Then he took them both apart, and said unto them, Bless God, praise him, and magnify him, and praise him for the things which he hath done unto you in the sight of all that live. It is good to praise God, and exalt his name, and honourably to shew forth the works of God; therefore be not slack to praise him. [7] It is good to keep close the secret of a king, but it is honourable to reveal the works of God. Do that which is good, and no evil shall touch you. [8] Prayer is good with fasting and alms and righteousness. A little with righteousness is better than much with unrighteousness. It is better to give alms than to lay up gold: [9] For alms doth deliver from death, and shall purge away all sin. Those that exercise alms and righteousness shall be filled with life: [10] But they that sin are enemies to their own life. [11] Surely I will keep close nothing from you. For I said, It was good to keep close the secret of a king, but that it was honourable to reveal the works of God. [12] Now therefore, when thou didst pray, and Sara thy daughter in law, I

did bring the remembrance of your prayers before the Holy One: and when thou didst bury the dead, I was with thee likewise. [13] And when thou didst not delay to rise up, and leave thy dinner, to go and cover the dead, thy good deed was not hid from me: but I was with thee. [14] And now God hath sent me to heal thee and Sara thy daughter in law. [15] I am Raphael, one of the seven holy angels, which present the prayers of the saints, and which go in and out before the glory of the Holy One. [16] Then they were both troubled, and fell upon their faces: for they feared. [17] But he said unto them, Fear not, for it shall go well with you; praise God therefore. [18] For not of any favour of mine, but by the will of our God I came; wherefore praise him for ever. [19] All these days I did appear unto you; but I did neither eat nor drink, but ye did see a vision. [20] Now therefore give God thanks: for I go up to him that sent me; but write all things which are done in a book. [21] And when they arose, they saw him no more. [22] Then they confessed the great and wonderful works of God, and how the angel of the Lord had appeared unto them.

13 [1] Then Tobit wrote a prayer of rejoicing, and said, Blessed be God that liveth for ever, and blessed be his kingdom. [2] For he doth scourge, and hath mercy: he leadeth down to hell, and bringeth up again: neither is there any that can avoid his hand. [3] Confess him before the Gentiles, ye children of Israel: for he hath scattered us among them. [4] There declare his greatness, and extol him before all the living: for he is our Lord, and he is the God our Father for ever. [5] And he will scourge us for our iniquities, and will have mercy again, and will gather us out of all nations, among whom he hath scattered us. [6] If ye turn to him with your whole heart, and

with your whole mind, and deal uprightly before him, then will he turn unto you, and will not hide his face from you. Therefore see what he will do with you, and confess him with your whole mouth, and praise the Lord of might, and extol the everlasting King. In the land of my captivity do I praise him, and declare his might and majesty to a sinful nation. O ye sinners, turn and do justice before him: who can tell if he will accept you, and have mercy on you? [7] I will extol my God, and my soul shall praise the King of heaven, and shall rejoice in his greatness. [8] Let all men speak, and let all praise him for his righteousness. [9] O Jerusalem, the holy city, he will scourge thee for thy children's works, and will have mercy again on the sons of the righteous. [10] Give praise to the Lord, for he is good: and praise the everlasting King, that his tabernacle may be builded in thee again with joy, and let him make joyful there in thee those that are captives, and love in thee for ever those that are miserable. [11] Many nations shall come from far to the name of the Lord God with gifts in their hands, even gifts to the King of heaven; all generations shall praise thee with great joy. [12] Cursed are all they which hate thee, and blessed shall all be which love thee for ever. [13] Rejoice and be glad for the children of the just: for they shall be gathered together, and shall bless the Lord of the just. [14] O blessed are they which love thee, for they shall rejoice in thy peace: blessed are they which have been sorrowful for all thy scourges; for they shall rejoice for thee, when they have seen all thy glory, and shall be glad for ever. [15] Let my soul bless God the great King. [16] For Jerusalem shall be built up with sapphires and emeralds, and precious stone: thy walls and towers and battlements with pure gold. [17] And the streets of Jerusalem shall be paved with beryl and carbuncle and stones of Ophir. [18] And all her streets shall say, Alleluia; and they shall praise him, saying, Blessed be God, which hath extolled it for ever.

14

[1] So Tobit made an end of praising God. [2] And he was eight and fifty years old when he lost his sight, which was restored to him after eight years: and he gave alms, and he increased in the fear of the Lord God, and praised him. [3] And when he was very aged he called his son, and the sons of his son, and said to him, My son, take thy children; for, behold, I am aged, and am ready to depart out of this life. [4] Go into Media my son, for I surely believe those things which Jonas the prophet spake of Nineve, that it shall be overthrown; and that for a time peace shall rather be in Media; and that our brethren shall lie scattered in the earth from that good land: and Jerusalem shall be desolate, and the house of God in it shall be burned, and shall be desolate for a time; [5] And that again God will have mercy on them, and bring them again into the land, where they shall build a temple, but not like to the first, until the time of that age be fulfilled; and afterward they shall return from all places of their captivity, and build up Jerusalem gloriously, and the house of God shall be built in it for ever with a glorious building, as the prophets have spoken thereof. [6] And all nations shall turn, and fear the Lord God truly, and shall bury their idols. [7] So shall all nations praise the Lord, and his people shall confess God, and the Lord shall exalt his people; and all those which love the Lord God in truth and justice shall rejoice, shewing mercy to our brethren. [8] And now, my son, depart out of Nineve, because that those things which the prophet Jonas spake shall surely come to pass. [9] But keep thou the law and the commandments,

and shew thyself merciful and just, that it may go well with thee. [10] And bury me decently, and thy mother with me; but tarry no longer at Nineve. Remember, my son, how Aman handled Achiacharus that brought him up, how out of light he brought him into darkness, and how he rewarded him again: yet Achiacharus was saved, but the other had his reward: for he went down into darkness. Manasses gave alms, and escaped the snares of death which they had set for him: but Aman fell into the snare, and perished. [11] Wherefore now, my son, consider what alms doeth, and how righteousness doth deliver. When he had said these things, he gave up the ghost in the bed, being an hundred and eight and fifty years old; and he buried him honourably. [12] And when Anna his mother was dead, he buried her with his father. But Tobias departed with his wife and children to Ecbatane to Raguel his father in law, [13] Where he became old with honour, and he buried his father and mother in law honourably, and he inherited their substance, and his father Tobit's. [14] And he died at Ecbatane in Media, being an hundred and seven and twenty years old. [15] But before he died he heard of the destruction of Nineve, which was taken by Nabuchodonosor and Assuerus: and before his death he rejoiced over Nineve.

THE BOOK OF JUDITH

1 [1] In the twelfth year of the reign of Nabuchodonosor, who reigned in Nineve, the great city; in the days of Arphaxad, which reigned over the Medes in Ecbatane, [2] and built in Ecbatane walls round about of stones hewn three cubits broad and six cubits long, and made the height of the wall seventy cubits, and the breadth thereof fifty cubits: [3] and set the towers thereof upon the gates of it, an hundred cubits high, and the breadth thereof in the foundation threescore cubits: [4] And he made the gates thereof, even gates that were raised to the height of seventy cubits, and the breadth of them was forty cubits, for the going forth of his mighty armies, and for the setting in array of his footmen: [5] Even in those days king Nabuchodonosor made war with king Arphaxad in the great plain, which is the plain in the borders of Ragau. [6] And there came unto him all they that dwelt in the hill country, and all they that dwelt by Euphrates, and Tigris, and Hydaspes, and the plain of Arioch the king of the Elymeans, and very many nations of the sons of Chelod, assembled themselves to the battle. [7] Then Nabuchodonosor king of

the Assyrians sent unto all that dwelt in Persia, and to all that dwelt westward, and to those that dwelt in Cilicia, and Damascus, and Libanus, and Antilibanus, and to all that dwelt upon the sea coast, [8] and to those among the nations that were of Carmel, and Galaad, and the higher Galilee, and the great plain of Esdrelom, [9] and to all that were in Samaria and the cities thereof, and beyond Jordan unto Jerusalem, and Betana, and Chellus, and Kades; and the river of Egypt, and Taphnes, and Ramesse, and all the land of Gesem, [10] until ye come beyond Tanis and Memphis, and to all the inhabitants of Egypt, until ye come to the borders of Ethiopia. [11] But all the inhabitants of the land made light of the commandment of Nabuchodonosor king of the Assyrians, neither went they with him to the battle; for they were not afraid of him: yea, he was before them as one man, and they sent away his ambassadors from them without effect, and with disgrace. [12] Therefore Nabuchodonosor was very angry with all this country, and sware by his throne and kingdom, that he would surely be avenged upon all those coasts of Cilicia, and Damascus, and Syria, and that he would slay with the sword all the inhabitants of the land of Moab, and the children of Ammon, and all Judea, and all that were in Egypt, till ye come to the borders of the two seas. [13] Then he marched in battle array with his power against king Arphaxad in the seventeenth year, and he prevailed in his battle; for he overthrew all the power of Arphaxad, and all his horsemen, and all his chariots, [14] and became lord of his cities, and came unto Ecbatane, and took the towers, and spoiled the streets thereof, and turned the beauty thereof into shame. [15] He took also Arphaxad in the mountains of Ragau, and smote him through with his darts, and destroyed him utterly that day. [16] So he returned afterward to Nineve, both he and all his company of sundry nations being a very great multitude of men of war, and there he took his ease, and banqueted, both he and his army, an hundred and twenty days.

2 [1] And in the eighteenth year, the two and twentieth day of the first month, there was talk in the house of Nabuchodonosor king of the Assyrians that he should, as he said, avenge himself on all the earth. [2] So he called unto him all his officers, and all his nobles, and communicated with them his secret counsel, and concluded the afflicting of the whole earth out of his own mouth. [3] Then they decreed to destroy all flesh that did not obey the commandment of his mouth. [4] And when he had ended his counsel, Nabuchodonosor king of the Assyrians called Holofernes the chief captain of his army, which was next unto him, and said unto him, [5] Thus saith the great king, the lord of the whole earth, Behold, thou shalt go forth from my presence, and take with thee men that trust in their own strength, of footmen an hundred and twenty thousand; and the number of horses with their riders twelve thousand. [6] And thou shalt go against all the west country, because they disobeyed my commandment. [7] And thou shalt declare unto them, that they prepare for me earth and water: for I will go forth in my wrath against them, and will cover the whole face of the earth with the feet of mine army, and I will give them for a spoil unto them: [8] so that their slain shall fill their valleys and brooks, and the river shall be filled with their dead, till it overflow: [9] And I will lead them captives to the utmost parts of all the earth. [10] Thou therefore shalt go forth, and take beforehand for me all their coasts: and if they will yield

themselves unto thee, thou shalt reserve them for me till the day of their punishment. [11] But concerning them that rebel, let not thine eye spare them; but put them to the slaughter, and spoil them wheresoever thou goest. [12] For as I live, and by the power of my kingdom, whatsoever I have spoken, that will I do by my hand. [13] And take thou heed that thou transgress none of the commandments of thy lord, but accomplish them fully, as I have commanded thee, and defer not to them. [14] Then Holofernes went forth from the presence of his lord, and called all the governors and captains, and the officers of the army of Assur; [15] and he mustered the chosen men for the battle, as his lord had commanded him, unto an hundred and twenty thousand, and twelve thousand archers on horseback; [16] and he ranged them, as a great army is ordered for the war. [17] And he took camels and asses for their carriages, a very great number; and sheep, and oxen, and goats without number for their provision: [18] and plenty of victual for every man of the army, and very much gold and silver out of the king's house. [19] Then he went forth and all his power to go before king Nabuchodonosor in the voyage, and to cover all the face of the earth westward with their chariots, and horsemen, and their chosen footmen. [20] A great number also of sundry countries came with them like locusts, and like the sand of the earth: for the multitude was without number. [21] And they went forth of Nineve three days' journey toward the plain of Bectileth, and pitched from Bectileth near the mountain which is at the left hand of the upper Cilicia. [22] Then he took all his army, his footmen, and horsemen, and chariots, and went from thence into the hill country; [23] and destroyed Phud and Lud, and spoiled all the children of Rasses, and the children of Ismael, which were toward the wilderness at the south of the land of the Chellians. [24] Then he went over Euphrates, and went through Mesopotamia, and destroyed all the high cities that were upon the river Arbonai, till ye come to the sea. [25] And he took the borders of Cilicia, and killed all that resisted him, and came to the borders of Japheth, which were towards the south, over against Arabia. [26] He compassed also all the children of Madian, and burned up their tabernacles, and spoiled their sheepcotes. [27] Then he went down into the plain of Damascus in the time of wheat harvest, and burned up all their fields, and destroyed their flocks and herds, also he spoiled their cities, and utterly wasted their countries, and smote all their young men with the edge of the sword. [28] Therefore the fear and dread of him fell upon all the inhabitants of the sea coasts, which were in Sidon and Tyrus, and them that dwelt in Sur and Ocina, and all that dwelt in Jemnaan; and they that dwelt in Azotus and Ascalon feared him greatly.

3 [1] So they sent ambassadors unto him to treat of peace, saying, [2] Behold, we the servants of Nabuchodonosor the great king lie before thee; use us as shall be good in thy sight. [3] Behold, our houses, and all our places, and all our fields of wheat, and flocks, and herds, and all the lodges of our tents, lie before thy face; use them as it pleaseth thee. [4] Behold, even our cities and the inhabitants thereof are thy servants; come and deal with them as seemeth good unto thee. [5] So the men came to Holofernes, and declared unto him after this manner. [6] Then came he down toward the sea coast, both he and his army, and set garrisons in the high cities, and took out of them chosen men for aid. [7] So they and all

the country round about received them with garlands, with dances, and with timbrels. [8] Yet he did cast down their frontiers, and cut down their groves: for he had decreed to destroy all the gods of the land, that all nations should worship Nabuchodonosor only, and that all tongues and tribes should call upon him as god. [9] Also he came over against Esdraelon near unto Judea, over against the great strait of Judea. [10] And he pitched between Geba and Sethopolis, and there he tarried a whole month, that he might gather together all the carriages of his army.

4 [1] Now the children of Israel that dwelt in Judea, heard all that Holofernes the chief captain of Nabuchodonosor king of the Assyrians had done to the nations, and after what manner he had spoiled all their temples, and brought them to nought. [2] Therefore they were exceedingly afraid of him, and were troubled for Jerusalem, and for the temple of the Lord their God: [3] For they were newly returned from the captivity, and all the people of Judea were lately gathered together: and the vessels, and the altar, and the house, were sanctified after the profanation. [4] Therefore they sent into all the coasts of Samaria and the villages, and the Bethoron, and Belmen, and Jericho, and to Choba and Esora, and to the valley of Salem: [5] and possessed themselves beforehand of all the tops of the high mountains, and fortified the villages that were in them, and laid up victuals for the provision of war: for their fields were of late reaped. [6] Also Joacim the high priest, which was in those days in Jerusalem, wrote to them that dwelt in Bethulia, and Betomestham, which is over against Esdraelon toward the open country, near to Dothaim, [7] charging them to keep the passages of the hill country:

for by them there was an entrance into Judea, and it was easy to stop them that would come up, because the passage was strait, for two men at the most. [8] And the children of Israel did as Joacim the high priest had commanded them, with the ancients of all the people of Israel, which dwelt at Jerusalem. [9] Then every man of Israel cried to God with great fervency, and with great vehemency did they humble their souls: [10] Both they, and their wives, and their children, and their cattle, and every stranger and hireling, and their servants bought with money, put sackcloth upon their loins. [11] Thus every man and woman, and the little children, and the inhabitants of Jerusalem, fell before the temple, and cast ashes upon their heads, and spread out their sackcloth before the face of the Lord; also they put sackcloth about the altar, [12] and cried to the God of Israel all with one consent earnestly, that he would not give their children for a prey, and their wives for a spoil, and the cities of their inheritance to destruction, and the sanctuary to profanation and reproach, and for the nations to rejoice at. [13] So God heard their prayers, and looked upon their afflictions: for the people fasted many days in all Judea and Jerusalem before the sanctuary of the Lord Almighty. [14] And Joacim the high priest, and all the priests that stood before the Lord, and they which ministered unto the Lord, had their loins girt with sackcloth, and offered the daily burnt offerings, with the vows and free gifts of the people, [15] and had ashes on their mitres, and cried unto the Lord with all their power, that he would look upon all the house of Israel graciously.

5 [1] Then was it declared to Holofernes, the chief captain of the army of Assur, that the children of Israel had pre-

pared for war, and had shut up the passages of the hill country, and had fortified all the tops of the high hills, and had laid impediments in the champaign countries: [2] Wherewith he was very angry, and called all the princes of Moab, and the captains of Ammon, and all the governors of the sea coast, [3] and he said unto them, Tell me now, ye sons of Chanaan, who this people is that dwelleth in the hill country, and what are the cities that they inhabit, and what is the multitude of their army, and wherein is their power and strength, and what king is set over them, or captain of their army; [4] and why have they determined not to come and meet me, more than all the inhabitants of the west. [5] Then said Achior, the captain of all the sons of Ammon, Let my lord now hear a word from the mouth of thy servant, and I will declare unto thee the truth concerning this people, which dwelleth near thee, and inhabiteth the hill countries: and there shall no lie come out of the mouth of thy servant. [6] This people are descended of the Chaldeans: [7] and they sojourned heretofore in Mesopotamia, because they would not follow the gods of their fathers, which were in the land of Chaldea. [8] For they left the way of their ancestors, and worshipped the God of heaven, the God whom they knew: so they cast them out from the face of their gods, and they fled into Mesopotamia, and sojourned there many days. [9] Then their God commanded them to depart from the place where they sojourned, and to go into the land of Chanaan: where they dwelt, and were increased with gold and silver, and with very much cattle. [10] But when a famine covered all the land of Chanaan, they went down into Egypt, and sojourned there, while they were nourished, and became there a great multitude, so that one could not number their nation. [11] Therefore the king of Egypt rose up against them, and dealt subtilly with them, and brought them low with labouring in brick, and made them slaves. [12] Then they cried unto their God, and he smote all the land of Egypt with incurable plagues: so the Egyptians cast them out of their sight. [13] And God dried the Red sea before them, [14] and brought them to mount Sina, and Cades-Barne, and cast forth all that dwelt in the wilderness. [15] So they dwelt in the land of the Amorites, and they destroyed by their strength all them of Esebon, and passing over Jordan they possessed all the hill country. [16] And they cast forth before them the Chanaanite, the Pherezite, the Jebusite, and the Sychemite, and all the Gergesites, and they dwelt in that country many days. [17] And whilst they sinned not before their God, they prospered, because the God that hateth iniquity was with them. [18] But when they departed from the way which he appointed them, they were destroyed in many battles very sore, and were led captives into a land that was not theirs, and the temple of their God was cast to the ground, and their cities were taken by the enemies. [19] But now are they returned to their God, and are come up from the places where they were scattered, and have possessed Jerusalem, where their sanctuary is, and are seated in the hill country; for it was desolate. [20] Now therefore, my lord and governor, if there be any error in this people, and they sin against their God, let us consider that this shall be their ruin, and let us go up, and we shall overcome them. [21] But if there be no iniquity in their nation, let my lord now pass by, lest their Lord defend them, and their God be for them, and we become a reproach before all the world. [22] And when Achior had finished these sayings, all the people standing round about the tent murmured, and the chief men of Holofernes, and all that dwelt by the sea side, and in Moab, spake that he should kill him. [23] For, say they, we will not be afraid of the face of the children of Israel: for, lo, it is a people that have no strength nor power for a strong battle. [24] Now therefore, lord Holofernes, we will go up, and they shall be a prey to be devoured of all thine army.

6 [1] And when the tumult of men that were about the council was ceased, Holofernes the chief captain of the army of Assur said unto Achior and all the Moabites before all the company of other nations, [2] and who art thou, Achior, and the hirelings of Ephraim, that thou hast prophesied among us as to-day, and hast said, that we should not make war with the people of Israel, because their God will defend them? and who is God but Nabuchodonosor? [3] He will send his power, and will destroy them from the face of the earth, and their God shall not deliver them: but we his servants will destroy them as one man; for they are not able to sustain the power of our horses. [4] For with them we will tread them under foot, and their mountains shall be drunken with their blood, and their fields shall be filled with their dead bodies, and their footsteps shall not be able to stand before us, for they shall utterly perish, saith king Nabuchodonosor, lord of all the earth: for he said, None of my words shall be in vain. [5] And thou, Achior, an hireling of Ammon, which hast spoken these words in the day of thine iniquity, shalt see my face no more from this day, until I take vengeance of this nation that came out of Egypt. [6] And then shall the sword of mine army, and the multitude of them that serve me, pass through thy sides, and thou shalt fall

among their slain, when I return. [7] Now therefore my servants shall bring thee back into the hill country, and shall set thee in one of the cities of the passages. [8] And thou shalt not perish, till thou be destroyed with them. [9] And if thou persuade thyself in thy mind that they shall not be taken, let not thy countenance fall: I have spoken it, and none of my words shall be in vain. [10] Then Holofernes commanded his servants, that waited in his tent, to take Achior, and bring him to Bethulia, and deliver him into the hands of the children of Israel. [11] So his servants took him, and brought him out of the camp into the plain, and they went from the midst of the plain into the hill country, and came unto the fountains that were under Bethulia. [12] And when the men of the city saw them, they took up their weapons, and went out of the city to the top of the hill: and every man that used a sling kept them from coming up by casting of stones against them. [13] Nevertheless, having gotten privily under the hill, they bound Achior, and cast him down, and left him at the foot of the hill, and returned to their lord. [14] But the Israelites descended from their city, and came unto him, and loosed him, and brought him to Bethulia, and presented him to the governors of the city: [15] which were in those days Ozias the son of Micha, of the tribe of Simeon, and Chabris the son of Gothonial, and Charmis the son of Melchiel. [16] And they called together all the ancients of the city, and all their youth ran together, and their women, to the assembly, and they set Achior in the midst of all their people. Then Ozias asked him of that which was done. [17] And he answered and declared unto them the words of the council of Holofernes, and all the words that he had spoken in the midst of the princes of Assur, and whatsoever Holofernes had spoken proudly against the house of Israel. [18] Then the people fell down and worshipped God, and cried unto God, saying, [19] O Lord God of heaven, behold their pride, and pity the low estate of our nation, and look upon the face of those that are sanctified unto thee this day. [20] Then they comforted Achior, and praised him greatly. [21] And Ozias took him out of the assembly unto his house, and made a feast to the elders; and they called on the God of Israel all that night for help.

7 [1] The next day Holofernes commanded all his army, and all his people which were come to take his part, that they should remove their camp against Bethulia, to take aforehand the ascents of the hill country, and to make war against the children of Israel. [2] Then their strong men removed their camps in that day, and the army of the men of war was an hundred and seventy thousand footmen, and twelve thousand horsemen, besides the baggage, and other men that were afoot among them, a very great multitude. [3] And they camped in the valley near unto Bethulia, by the fountain, and they spread themselves in breadth over Dothaim even to Belmaim, and in length from Bethulia unto Cyamon, which is over against Esdraelon. [4] Now the children of Israel, when they saw the multitude of them, were greatly troubled, and said every one to his neighbour, Now will these men lick up the face of the earth; for neither the high mountains, nor the valleys, nor the hills, are able to bear their weight. [5] Then every man took up his weapons of war, and when they had kindled fires upon their towers, they remained and watched all that night. [6] But in the second day Holofernes brought forth all his horsemen

in the sight of the children of Israel which were in Bethulia; [7] and viewed the passages up to the city, and came to the fountains of their waters, and took them, and set garrisons of men of war over them, and he himself removed toward his people. [8] Then came unto him all the chief of the children of Esau, and all the governors of the people of Moab, and the captains of the sea coast, and said, [9] Let our lord now hear a word, that there be not an overthrow in thine army. [10] For this people of the children of Israel do not trust in their spears, but in the height of the mountains wherein they dwell, because it is not easy to come up to the tops of their mountains. [11] Now therefore, my lord, fight not against them in battle array, and there shall not so much as one man of thy people perish. [12] Remain in thy camp, and keep all the men of thine army, and let thy servants get into their hands the fountain of water, which issueth forth of the foot of the mountain: [13] For all the inhabitants of Bethulia have their water thence: so shall thirst kill them, and they shall give up their city, and we and our people shall go up to the tops of the mountains that are near, and will camp upon them, to watch that none go out of the city. [14] So they and their wives and their children shall be consumed with famine, and before the sword come against them, they shall be overthrown in the streets where they dwell. [15] Thus shalt thou render them an evil reward; because they rebelled, and met not thy person peaceably. [16] And these words pleased Holofernes and all his servants, and he appointed to do as they had spoken. [17] So the camp of the children of Ammon departed, and with them five thousand of the Assyrians, and they pitched in the valley, and took the waters, and the fountains of the waters of the children of Israel. [18] Then the children of Esau went up with the children of Ammon, and camped in the hill country over against Dothaim: and they sent some of them toward the south, and toward the east, over against Ekrebel, which is near unto Chusi, that is upon the brook Mochmur; and the rest of the army of the Assyrians camped in the plain, and covered the face of the whole land; and their tents and carriages were pitched to a very great multitude. [19] Then the children of Israel cried unto the Lord their God, because their heart failed, for all their enemies had compassed them round about, and there was no way to escape out from among them. [20] Thus all the company of Assur remained about them, both their footmen, chariots, and horsemen, four and thirty days, so that all their vessels of water failed all the inhabitants of Bethulia. [21] And the cisterns were emptied, and they had not water to drink their fill for one day; for they gave them drink by measure. [22] Therefore their young children were out of heart, and their women and young men fainted for thirst, and fell down in the streets of the city, and by the passages of the gates, and there was no longer any strength in them. [23] Then all the people assembled to Ozias, and to the chief of the city, both young men, and women, and children, and cried with a loud voice, and said before all the elders, [24] God be judge between us and you: for ye have done us great injury, in that ye have not required peace of the children of Assur. [25] For now we have no helper: but God hath sold us into their hands, that we should be thrown down before them with thirst and great destruction. [26] Now therefore call them unto you, and deliver the whole city for a spoil to the people of Holofernes, and to all his army. [27] For it is better for us to be made a spoil unto them, than to die for thirst: for we will be his servants, that our souls may live, and not see the death of our infants before our eyes, nor our wives nor our children to die. [28] We take to witness against you the heaven and the earth, and our God and Lord of our fathers, which punisheth us according to our sins and the sins of our fathers, that he do not according as we have said this day. [29] Then there was great weeping with one consent in the midst of the assembly; and they cried unto the Lord God with a loud voice. [30] Then said Ozias to them, Brethren, be of good courage, let us yet endure five days, in the which space the Lord our God may turn his mercy towards us; for he will not forsake us utterly. [31] And if these days pass, and there come no help unto us, I will do according to your word. [32] And he dispersed the people, every one to their own charge; and they went unto the walls and towers of their city, and sent the women and children into their houses: and they were very low brought in the city.

8 [1] Now at that time Judith heard thereof, which was the daughter of Merari, the son of Ox, the son of Joseph, the son of Oziel, the son of Elcia, the son of Ananias, the son of Gideon, the son of Raphaim, the son of Acitho, the son of Eliu, the son of Eliab, the son of Nathaneel, the son of Samael, the son of Salasadai, the son of Israel. [2] And Manasses was her husband, of her tribe and kindred, who died in the barley harvest. [3] For as he stood overseeing them that bound sheaves in the field, the heat came upon his head, and he fell on his bed, and died in the city of Bethulia: and they buried him with his fathers in the field between Dothaim and Balamo. [4] So Judith was a widow in her house three years and four months. [5] And she made her a tent upon

the top of her house, and put on sackcloth upon her loins, and ware her widow's apparel. [6] And she fasted all the days of her widowhood, save the eves of the sabbaths, and the sabbaths, and the eves of the new moons, and the new moons, and the feasts and solemn days of the house of Israel. [7] She was also of a goodly countenance, and very beautiful to behold: and her husband Manasses had left her gold, and silver, and menservants, and maidservants, and cattle, and lands; and she remained upon them. [8] And there was none that gave her an ill word; for she feared God greatly. [9] Now when she heard the evil words of the people against the governor, that they fainted for lack of water; for Judith had heard all the words that Ozias had spoken unto them, and that he had sworn to deliver the city unto the Assyrians after five days; [10] then she sent her waitingwoman, that had the government of all things that she had, to call Ozias and Chabris and Charmis, the ancients of the city. [11] And they came unto her, and she said unto them, Hear me now, O ye governors of the inhabitants of Bethulia: for your words that ye have spoken before the people this day are not right, touching this oath which ye made and pronounced between God and you, and have promised to deliver the city to our enemies, unless within these days the Lord turn to help you. [12] And now who are ye that have tempted God this day, and stand instead of God among the children of men? [13] And now try the Lord Almighty, but ye shall never know any thing. [14] For ye cannot find the depth of the heart of man, neither can ye perceive the things that he thinketh; then how can ye search out God, that hath made all these things, and know his mind, or comprehend his purpose? Nay, my brethren, provoke not the Lord our God to anger. [15] For if he will not help us within these five days, he hath power to defend us when he will, even every day, or to destroy us before our enemies. [16] Do not bind the counsels of the Lord our God: for God is not as man, that he may be threatened; neither is he as the son of man, that he should be wavering. [17] Therefore let us wait for salvation of him, and call upon him to help us, and he will hear our voice, if it please him. [18] For there arose none in our age, neither is there any now in these days, neither tribe, nor family, nor people, nor city among us, which worship gods made with hands, as hath been aforetime. [19] For the which cause our fathers were given to the sword, and for a spoil, and had a great fall before our enemies. [20] But we know none other God, therefore we trust that he will not despise us, nor any of our nation. [21] For if we be taken so, all Judea shall lie waste, and our sanctuary shall be spoiled; and he will require the profanation thereof at our mouth. [22] And the slaughter of our brethren, and the captivity of the country, and the desolation of our inheritance, will he turn upon our heads among the Gentiles, wheresoever we shall be in bondage; and we shall be an offence and a reproach to all them that possess us. [23] For our servitude shall not be directed to favour: but the Lord our God shall turn it to dishonour. [24] Now therefore, O brethren, let us shew an example to our brethren, because their hearts depend upon us, and the sanctuary, and the house, and the altar, rest upon us. [25] Moreover, let us give thanks to the Lord our God, which trieth us, even as he did our fathers. [26] Remember what things he did to Abraham, and how he tried Isaac, and what happened to Jacob in Mesopotamia of Syria, when he kept the sheep of Laban his mother's brother. [27] For he hath not tried us in the fire, as he did them, for the examination of their hearts, neither hath he taken vengeance on us: but the Lord doth scourge them that come near unto him, to admonish them. [28] Then said Ozias to her, All that thou hast spoken, hast thou spoken with a good heart, and there is none that may gainsay thy words. [29] For this is not the first day wherein thy wisdom is manifested; but from the beginning of thy days all the people have known thy understanding, because the disposition of thine heart is good. [30] But the people were very thirsty, and compelled us to do unto them as we have spoken, and to bring an oath upon ourselves, which we will not break. [31] Therefore now pray thou for us, because thou art a godly woman, and the Lord will send us rain to fill our cisterns, and we shall faint no more. [32] Then said Judith unto them, Hear me, and I will do a thing which shall go throughout all generations to the children of our nation. [33] Ye shall stand this night in the gate, and I will go forth with my waiting-woman: and within the days that ye have promised to deliver the city to our enemies, the Lord will visit Israel by mine hand. [34] But enquire not ye of mine act: for I will not declare it unto you, till the things be finished that I do. [35] Then said Ozias and the princes unto her, Go in peace, and the Lord God be before thee, to take vengeance on our enemies. [36] So they returned from the tent, and went to their wards.

9 [1] Judith fell upon her face, and put ashes upon her head, and uncovered the sackcloth wherewith she was clothed; and about the time that the incense of that evening was offered in Jerusalem in the house of the Lord, Judith cried with a loud voice, and said, [2] O Lord God of my father Simeon, to whom thou gavest a sword to take vengeance of the strangers, who loosened the

girdle of a maid to defile her, and discovered the thigh to her shame, and polluted her virginity to her reproach; for thou saidst, It shall not be so; and yet they did so: [3] Wherefore thou gavest their rulers to be slain, so that they dyed their bed in blood, being deceived, and smotest the servants with their lords, and the lords upon their thrones; [4] and hast given their wives for a prey, and their daughters to be captives, and all their spoils to be divided among thy dear children; which were moved with thy zeal, and abhorred the pollution of their blood, and called upon thee for aid: O God, O my God, hear me also a widow. [5] For thou hast wrought not only those things, but also the things which fell out before, and which ensued after; thou hast thought upon the things which are now, and which are to come. [6] Yea, what things thou didst determine were ready at hand, and said, Lo, we are here: for all thy ways are prepared, and thy judgments are in thy foreknowledge. [7] For, behold, the Assyrians are multiplied in their power; they are exalted with horse and man; they glory in the strength of their footmen; they trust in shield, and spear, and bow, and sling; and know not that thou art the Lord that breakest the battles: the Lord is thy name. [8] Throw down their strength in thy power, and bring down their force in thy wrath: for they have purposed to defile thy sanctuary, and to pollute the tabernacle where thy glorious name resteth, and to cast down with the sword the horn of thine altar. [9] Behold their pride, and send thy wrath upon their heads: give into mine hand, which am a widow, the power that I have conceived. [10] Smite by the deceit of my lips the servant with the prince, and the prince with the servant; break down their stateliness by the hand of a woman. [11] For thy power standeth not in multitude, nor thy might in strong men: for thou art a God of the afflicted, an helper of the oppressed, an upholder of the weak, a protector of the forlorn, a saviour of them that are without hope. [12] I pray thee, I pray thee, O God of my father, and God of the inheritance of Israel, Lord of the heavens and earth, Creator of the waters, King of every creature, hear thou my prayer: [13] And make my speech and deceit to be their wound and stripe, who have purposed cruel things against thy covenant, and thy hallowed house, and against the top of Sion, and against the house of the possession of thy children. [14] And make every nation and tribe to acknowledge that thou art the God of all power and might, and that there is none other that protecteth the people of Israel but thou.

10 [1] Now after that she had ceased to cry unto the God of Israel, and had made an end of all these words, [2] she rose where she had fallen down, and called her maid, and went down into the house in which she abode in the sabbath days, and in her feast days, [3] and pulled off the sackcloth which she had on, and put off the garments of her widowhood, and washed her body all over with water, and anointed herself with precious ointment, and braided the hair of her head, and put on a tire upon it, and put on her garments of gladness, wherewith she was clad during the life of Manasses her husband. [4] And she took sandals upon her feet, and put about her her bracelets, and her chains, and her rings, and her earrings, and all her ornaments, and decked herself bravely, to allure the eyes of all men that should see her. [5] Then she gave her maid a bottle of wine, and a cruse of oil, and filled a bag with parched corn, and lumps of figs, and with fine bread; so she folded all these

things together, and laid them upon her. [6] Thus they went forth to the gate of the city of Bethulia, and found standing there Ozias and the ancients of the city, Chabris and Charmis. [7] And when they saw her, that her countenance was altered, and her apparel was changed, they wondered at her beauty very greatly, and said unto her, [8] The God, the God of our fathers give thee favour, and accomplish thine enterprises to the glory of the children of Israel, and to the exaltation of Jerusalem. Then they worshipped God. [9] And she said unto them, Command the gates of the city to be opened unto me, that I may go forth to accomplish the things whereof ye have spoken with me. So they commanded the young men to open unto her, as she had spoken. [10] And when they had done so, Judith went out, she, and her maid with her; and the men of the city looked after her, until she was gone down the mountain, and till she had passed the valley, and could see her no more. [11] Thus they went straight forth in the valley: and the first watch of the Assyrians met her, [12] and took her, and asked her, Of what people art thou? and whence comest thou? and whither goest thou? And she said, I am a woman of the Hebrews, and am fled from them: for they shall be given you to be consumed: [13] And I am coming before Holofernes the chief captain of your army, to declare words of truth; and I will shew him a way, whereby he shall go, and win all the hill country, without losing the body or life of any one of his men. [14] Now when the men heard her words, and beheld her countenance, they wondered greatly at her beauty, and said unto her, [15] Thou hast saved thy life, in that thou hast hasted to come down to the presence of our lord: now therefore come to his tent, and some of us shall conduct thee, until they have delivered thee to his hands. [16] And when thou standest before him, be not afraid in thine heart, but shew unto him according to thy word; and he will entreat thee well. [17] Then they chose out of them an hundred men to accompany her and her maid; and they brought her to the tent of Holofernes. [18] Then was there a concourse throughout all the camp: for her coming was noised among the tents, and they came about her, as she stood without the tent of Holofernes, till they told him of her. [19] And they wondered at her beauty, and admired the children of Israel because of her, and every one said to his neighbour, Who would despise this people, that have among them such women? surely it is not good that one man of them be left, who being let go might deceive the whole earth. [20] And they that lay near Holofernes went out, and all his servants, and they brought her into the tent. [21] Now Holofernes rested upon his bed under a canopy, which was woven with purple, and gold, and emeralds, and precious stones. [22] So they shewed him of her; and he came out before his tent with silver lamps going before him. [23] And when Judith was come before him and his servants, they all marvelled at the beauty of her countenance; and she fell down upon her face, and did reverence unto him: and his servants took her up.

11 [1] Then said Holofernes unto her, Woman, be of good comfort, fear not in thine heart: for I never hurt any that was willing to serve Nabuchodonosor, the king of all the earth. [2] Now therefore, if thy people that dwelleth in the mountains had not set light by me, I would not have lifted up my spear against them: but they have done these things to themselves. [3] But now tell me wherefore thou art fled from them, and art come

unto us: for thou art come for safeguard; be of good comfort, thou shalt live this night, and hereafter: [4] For none shall hurt thee, but entreat thee well, as they do the servants of king Nabuchodonosor my lord. [5] Then Judith said unto him, Receive the words of thy servant, and suffer thine handmaid to speak in thy presence, and I will declare no lie to my lord this night. [6] And if thou wilt follow the words of thine handmaid, God will bring the thing perfectly to pass by thee; and my lord shall not fail of his purposes. [7] As Nabuchodonosor king of all the earth liveth, and as his power liveth, who hath sent thee for the upholding of every living thing: for not only men shall serve him by thee, but also the beasts of the field, and the cattle, and the fowls of the air, shall live by thy power under Nabuchodonosor and all his house. [8] For we have heard of thy wisdom and thy policies, and it is reported in all the earth, that thou only art excellent in all the kingdom, and mighty in knowledge, and wonderful in feats of war. [9] Now as concerning the matter, which Achior did speak in thy council, we have heard his words; for the men of Bethulia saved him, and he declared unto them all that he had spoken unto thee. [10] Therefore, O lord and governor, reject not his word; but lay it up in thine heart, for it is true: for our nation shall not be punished, neither can the sword prevail against them, except they sin against their God. [11] And now, that my lord be not defeated and frustrate of his purpose, even death is now fallen upon them, and their sin hath overtaken them, wherewith they will provoke their God to anger, whensoever they shall do that which is not fit to be done: [12] For their victuals fail them, and all their water is scant, and they have determined to lay hands upon their cattle, and purposed to consume all those things, that God hath forbidden them to eat by his laws: [13] and are resolved to spend the firstfruits of the corn, and the tenths of wine and oil, which they had sanctified, and reserved for the priests that serve in Jerusalem before the face of our God; the which things it is not lawful for any of the people so much as to touch with their hands. [14] For they have sent some to Jerusalem, because they also that dwell there have done the like, to bring them a license from the senate. [15] Now when they shall bring them word, they will forthwith do it, and they shall be given to thee to be destroyed the same day. [16] Wherefore I thine handmaid, knowing all this, am fled from their presence; and God hath sent me to work things with thee, whereat all the earth shall be astonished, and whosoever shall hear it. [17] For thy servant is religious, and serveth the God of heaven day and night: now therefore, my lord, I will remain with thee, and thy servant will go out by night into the valley, and I will pray unto God, and he will tell me when they have committed their sins: [18] And I will come and shew it unto thee: then thou shalt go forth with all thine army, and there shall be none of them that shall resist thee. [19] And I will lead thee through the midst of Judea, until thou come before Jerusalem; and I will set thy throne in the midst thereof; and thou shalt drive them as sheep that have no shepherd, and a dog shall not so much as open his mouth at thee: for these things were told me according to my foreknowledge, and they were declared unto me, and I am sent to tell thee. [20] Then her words pleased Holofernes and all his servants; and they marvelled at her wisdom, and said, [21] There is not such a woman from one end of the earth to the other, both for beauty of face, and wisdom of words. [22] Likewise Holofernes said unto her, God hath done well to send thee before the people, that strength might be in our hands and destruction upon them that lightly regard my lord. [23] And now thou art both beautiful in thy countenance, and witty in thy words: surely if thou do as thou hast spoken, thy God shall be my God, and thou shalt dwell in the house of king Nabuchodonosor, and shalt be renowned through the whole earth.

12 [1] Then he commanded to bring her in where his plate was set; and bade that they should prepare for her of his own meats, and that she should drink of his own wine. [2] And Judith said, I will not eat thereof, lest there be an offence: but provision shall be made for me of the things that I have brought. [3] Then Holofernes said unto her, If thy provision should fail, how should we give thee the like? for there be none with us of thy nation. [4] Then said Judith unto him, As thy soul liveth, my lord, thine handmaid shall not spend those things that I have, before the Lord work by mine hand the things that he hath determined. [5] Then the servants of Holofernes brought her into the tent, and she slept till midnight, and she arose when it was toward the morning watch, [6] and sent to Holofernes, saying, Let my lord now command that thine handmaid may go forth unto prayer. [7] Then Holofernes commanded his guard that they should not stay her: thus she abode in the camp three days, and went out in the night into the valley of Bethulia, and washed herself in a fountain of water by the camp. [8] And when she came out, she besought the Lord God of Israel to direct her way to the raising up of the children of her people. [9] So she came in clean, and remained in the tent, until she did eat her meat at evening. [10] And in the fourth day Holofernes made a

feast to his own servants only, and called none of the officers to the banquet. [11] Then said he to Bagoas the eunuch, who had charge over all that he had, Go now, and persuade this Hebrew woman which is with thee, that she come unto us, and eat and drink with us. [12] For, lo, it will be a shame for our person, if we shall let such a woman go, not having had her company; for if we draw her not unto us, she will laugh us to scorn. [13] Then went Bagoas from the presence of Holofernes, and came to her, and he said, Let not this fair damsel fear to come to my lord, and to be honoured in his presence, and drink wine, and be merry with us, and be made this day as one of the daughters of the Assyrians, which serve in the house of Nabuchodonosor. [14] Then said Judith unto him, Who am I now, that I should gainsay my lord? surely whatsoever pleaseth him I will do speedily, and it shall be my joy unto the day of my death. [15] So she arose, and decked herself with her apparel and all her woman's attire, and her maid went and laid soft skins on the ground for her over against Holofernes, which she had received of Bagoas for her daily use, that she might sit and eat upon them. [16] Now when Judith came in and sat down, Holofernes' heart was ravished with her, and his mind was moved, and he desired greatly her company; for he waited a time to deceive her, from the day that he had seen her. [17] Then said Holofernes unto her, Drink now, and be merry with us. [18] So Judith said, I will drink now, my lord, because my life is magnified in me this day more than all the days since I was born. [19] Then she took and ate and drank before him what her maid had prepared. [20] And Holofernes took great delight in her, and drank more wine than he had drunk at any time in one day since he was born.

13 [1] Now when the evening was come, his servants made haste to depart, and Bagoas shut his tent without, and dismissed the waiters from the presence of his lord; and they went to their beds: for they were all weary, because the feast had been long. [2] And Judith was left alone in the tent, and Holofernes lying along upon his bed: for he was filled with wine. [3] Now Judith had commanded her maid to stand without her bedchamber, and to wait for her coming forth, as she did daily: for she said she would go forth to her prayers, and she spake to Bagoas according to the same purpose. [4] So all went forth, and none was left in the bedchamber, neither little nor great. Then Judith, standing by his bed, said in her heart, O Lord God of all power, look at this present upon the works of mine hands for the exaltation of Jerusalem. [5] For now is the time to help thine inheritance, and to execute thine enterprises to the destruction of the enemies which are risen against us. [6] Then she came to the pillar of the bed, which was at Holofernes' head, and took down his falchion from thence, [7] and approached to his bed, and took hold of the hair of his head, and said, Strengthen me, O Lord God of Israel, this day. [8] And she smote twice upon his neck with all her might, and she took away his head from him. [9] And tumbled his body down from the bed, and pulled down the canopy from the pillars, and anon after she went forth, and gave Holofernes' head to her maid; [10] and she put it in her bag of meat: so they twain went together according to their custom unto prayer: and when they passed the camp, they compassed the valley, and went up the mountain of Bethulia, and came to the gates thereof. [11] Then said Judith afar off, to the watchmen at the gate, Open, open now the gate: God, even our God, is with us, to shew his power yet in

Jerusalem, and his forces against the enemy, as he hath even done this day. [12] Now when the men of her city heard her voice, they made haste to go down to the gate of their city, and they called the elders of the city. [13] And then they ran all together, both small and great, for it was strange unto them that she was come: so they opened the gate, and received them, and made a fire for a light, and stood round about them. [14] Then she said to them with a loud voice, Praise, praise God, praise God, I say, for he hath not taken away his mercy from the house of Israel, but hath destroyed our enemies by mine hands this night. [15] So she took the head out of the bag, and shewed it, and said unto them, Behold the head of Holofernes, the chief captain of the army of Assur, and behold the canopy, wherein he did lie in his drunkenness; and the Lord hath smitten him by the hand of a woman. [16] As the Lord liveth, who hath kept me in my way that I went, my countenance hath deceived him to his destruction, and yet hath he not committed sin with me, to defile and shame me. [17] Then all the people were wonderfully astonished, and bowed themselves, and worshipped God, and said with one accord, Blessed be thou, O our God, which hast this day brought to nought the enemies of thy people. [18] Then said Ozias unto her, O daughter, blessed art thou of the most high God above all the women upon the earth; and blessed be the Lord God, which hath created the heavens and the earth, which hath directed thee to the cutting off of the head of the chief of our enemies. [19] For this thy confidence shall not depart from the heart of men, which remember the power of God for ever. [20] And God turn these things to thee for a perpetual praise, to visit thee in good things because thou hast not spared thy life for the affliction of our nation, but hast revenged our ruin, walking a straight way before our God. And all the people said, So be it, so be it.

14 [1] Then said Judith unto them, Hear me now, my brethren, and take this head, and hang it upon the highest place of your walls. [2] And so soon as the morning shall appear, and the sun shall come forth upon the earth, take ye every one his weapons, and go forth every valiant man out of the city, and set ye a captain over them, as though ye would go down into the field toward the watch of the Assyrians; but go not down. [3] Then they shall take their armour, and shall go into their camp, and raise up the captains of the army of Assur, and shall run to the tent of Holofernes, but shall not find him: then fear shall fall upon them, and they shall flee before your face. [4] So ye, and all that inhabit the coast of Israel, shall pursue them, and overthrow them as they go. [5] But before ye do these things, call me, Achior the Ammonite, that he may see and know him that despised the house of Israel, and that sent him to us, as it were to his death. [6] Then they called Achior out of the house of Ozias; and when he was come, and saw the head of Holofernes in a man's hand in the assembly of the people, he fell down on his face, and his spirit failed. [7] But when they had recovered him, he fell at Judith's feet, and reverenced her, and said, Blessed art thou in all the tabernacles of Juda, and in all nations, which hearing thy name shall be astonished. [8] Now therefore tell me all the things that thou hast done in these days. Then Judith declared unto him in the midst of the people all that she had done, from the

day that she went forth until that hour she spake unto them. [9] And when she had left off speaking, the people shouted with a loud voice, and made a joyful noise in their city. [10] And when Achior had seen all that the God of Israel had done, he believed in God greatly, and circumcised the flesh of his foreskin, and was joined unto the house of Israel unto this day. [11] And as soon as the morning arose, they hanged the head of Holofernes upon the wall, and every man took his weapons, and they went forth by bands unto the straits of the mountain. [12] But when the Assyrians saw them, they sent to their leaders, which came to their captains and tribunes, and to every one of their rulers. [13] So they came to Holofernes' tent, and said to him that had the charge of all his things, Waken now our lord: for the slaves have been bold to come down against us to battle, that they may be utterly destroyed. [14] Then went in Bagoas, and knocked at the door of the tent: for he thought that he had slept with Judith. [15] But because none answered, he opened it, and went into the bedchamber, and found him cast upon the floor dead, and his head was taken from him. [16] Therefore he cried with a loud voice, with weeping, and sighing, and a mighty cry, and rent his garments. [17] After, he went into the tent where Judith lodged: and when he found her not, he leaped out to the people, and cried, [18] These slaves have dealt treacherously; one woman of the Hebrews hath brought shame upon the house of king Nabuchodonosor: for, behold, Holofernes lieth upon the ground without a head. [19] When the captains of the Assyrians' army heard these words, they rent their coats and their minds were wonderfully troubled, and there was a cry and a very great noise throughout the camp.

15 [1] And when they that were in the tents heard, they were astonished at the thing that was done. [2] And fear and trembling fell upon them, so that there was no man that durst abide in the sight of his neighbour, but rushing out all together, they fled into every way of the plain, and of the hill country. [3] They also that had camped in the mountains round about Bethulia fled away. Then the children of Israel, every one that was a warrior among them, rushed out upon them. [4] Then sent Ozias to Betomasthem, and to Bebai, and Chobai, and Cola, and to all the coasts of Israel, such as should tell the things that were done, and that all should rush forth upon their enemies to destroy them. [5] Now when the children of Israel heard it, they all fell upon them with one consent, and slew them unto Chobai: likewise also they that came from Jerusalem, and from all the hill country, (for men had told them what things were done in the camp of their enemies,) and they that were in Galaad, and in Galilee, chased them with a great slaughter, until they were past Damascus and the borders thereof. [6] And the residue that dwelt at Bethulia, fell upon the camp of Assur, and spoiled them, and were greatly enriched. [7] And the children of Israel that returned from the slaughter had that which remained; and the villages and the cities, that were in the mountains and in the plain, gat many spoils: for the multitude was very great. [8] Then Joacim the high priest, and the ancients of the children of Israel that dwelt in Jerusalem, came to behold the good things that God had shewed to Israel, and to see Judith, and to salute her. [9] And when they came unto her, they blessed her with one accord, and said unto her, Thou art the exaltation of Jerusalem, thou art the great glory of Israel, thou art the great rejoicing of our nation: [10] Thou hast

done all these things by thine hand: thou hast done much good to Israel, and God is pleased therewith: blessed be thou of the Almighty Lord for evermore. And all the people said, So be it. [11] And the people spoiled the camp the space of thirty days: and they gave unto Judith Holofernes' tent, and all his plate, and beds, and vessels, and all his stuff: and she took it, and laid it on her mule; and made ready her carts, and laid them thereon. [12] Then all the women of Israel ran together to see her, and blessed her, and made a dance among them for her: and she took branches in her hand, and gave also to the women that were with her. [13] And they put a garland of olive upon her and her maid that was with her, and she went before all the people in the dance, leading all the women: and all the men of Israel followed in their armour with garlands, and with songs in their mouths.

16 [1] Then Judith began to sing this thanksgiving in all Israel, and all the people sang after her this song of praise. [2] And Judith said, Begin unto my God with timbrels, sing unto my Lord with cymbals: tune unto him a new psalm: exalt him, and call upon his name. [3] For God breaketh the battles: for among the camps in the midst of the people he hath delivered me out of the hands of them that persecuted me. [4] Assur came out of the mountains from the north, he came with ten thousands of his army, the multitude whereof stopped the torrents, and their horsemen have covered the hills. [5] He bragged that he would burn up my borders, and kill my young men with the sword, and dash the sucking children against the ground, and make mine infants as a prey, and my virgins as a spoil. [6] But the Almighty Lord hath disappointed them by the hand of a woman.

[7] For the mighty one did not fall by the young men, neither did the sons of the Titans smite him, nor high giants set upon him: but Judith, the daughter of Merari, weakened him with the beauty of her countenance. [8] For she put off the garment of her widowhood for the exaltation of those that were oppressed in Israel, and anointed her face with ointment, and bound her hair in a tire, and took a linen garment to deceive him. [9] Her sandals ravished his eyes, her beauty took his mind prisoner, and the falchion passed through his neck. [10] The Persians quaked at her boldness, and the Medes were daunted at her hardiness. [11] Then my afflicted shouted for joy, and my weak ones cried aloud; but they were astonished: these lifted up their voices, but they were overthrown. [12] The sons of the damsels have pierced them through, and wounded them as fugitives' children: they perished by the battle of the Lord. [13] I will sing unto the Lord a new song: O Lord, thou art great and glorious, wonderful in strength, and invincible. [14] Let all creatures serve thee: for thou spakest, and they were made, thou didst send forth thy spirit, and it created them, and there is none that can resist thy voice. [15] For the mountains shall be moved from their foundations with the waters, the rocks shall melt as wax at thy presence: yet thou art merciful to them that fear thee. [16] For all sacrifice is too little for a sweet savour unto thee, and all the fat is not sufficient for thy burnt offering: but he that feareth the Lord is great at all times. [17] Woe to the nations that rise up against my kindred! the Lord Almighty will take vengeance of them in the day of judgment, in putting fire and worms in their flesh; and they shall feel them, and weep for ever. [18] Now as soon as they entered into Jerusalem, they worshipped the Lord; and as soon as the people

were purified, they offered their burnt offerings, and their free offerings, and their gifts. [19] Judith also dedicated all the stuff of Holofernes, which the people had given her, and gave the canopy, which she had taken out of his bedchamber, for a gift unto the Lord. [20] So the people continued feasting in Jerusalem before the sanctuary for the space of three months, and Judith remained with them. [21] After this time every one returned to his own inheritance, and Judith went to Bethulia, and remained in her own possession, and was in her time honourable in all the country. [22] And many desired her, but none knew her all the days of her life, after that Manasses her husband was dead, and was gathered to his people. [23] But she increased more and more in honour, and waxed old in her husband's house, being an hundred and five years old, and made her maid free; so she died in Bethulia: and they buried her in the cave of her husband Manasses. [24] And the house of Israel lamented her seven days: and before she died, she did distribute her goods to all them that were nearest of kindred to Manasses her husband, and to them that were the nearest of her kindred. [25] And there was none that made the children of Israel any more afraid in the days of Judith, nor a long time after her death.

THE REST OF THE CHAPTERS OF THE BOOK OF ESTHER

10 [4] Then Mardocheus said, God hath done these things. [5] For I remember a dream which I saw concerning these matters, and nothing thereof hath failed. [6] A little fountain became a river, and there was light, and the sun, and much water: this river is Esther, whom the king married, and made queen. [7] And the two dragons are I and Aman. [8] And the nations were those that were assembled to destroy the name of the Jews: [9] And my nation is this Israel, which cried to God, and were saved: for the Lord hath saved his people, and the Lord hath delivered us from all those evils, and God hath wrought signs and great wonders, which have not been done among the Gentiles. [10] Therefore hath he made two lots, one for the people of God, and another for all the Gentiles. [11] And these two lots came at the hour, and time, and day of judgment, before God among all nations. [12] So God remembered his people, and justi-

fied his inheritance. [13] Therefore those days shall be unto them in the month Adar, the fourteenth and fifteenth day of the same month, with an assembly, and joy, and with gladness before God, according to the generations for ever among his people.

11 [1] In the fourth year of the reign of Ptolemeus and Cleopatra, Dositheus, who said he was a priest and Levite, and Ptolemeus his son, brought this epistle of Phurim, which they said was the same, and that Lysimachus the son of Ptolemeus, that was in Jerusalem, had interpreted it. [2] In the second year of the reign of Artaxerxes the great, in the first day of the month Nisan, Mardocheus the son of Jairus, the son of Semei, the son of Cisai, of the tribe of Benjamin, had a dream; [3] who was a Jew, and dwelt in the city of Susa, a great man, being a servitor in the king's court. [4] He was also one of the captives, which Nabuchodonosor the king of Babylon carried from Jerusalem with Jechonias king of Judea; and this was his dream: [5] Behold a noise of a tumult, with thunder, and earthquakes, and uproar in the land: [6] And, behold, two great dragons came forth ready to fight, and their cry was great. [7] And at their cry all nations were prepared to battle, that they might fight against the righteous people. [8] And lo, a day of darkness and obscurity, tribulation and anguish, affliction and great uproar, upon earth. [9] And the whole righteous nation was troubled, fearing their own evils, and were ready to perish. [10] Then they cried unto God, and upon their cry, as it were from a little fountain, was made a great flood, even much water. [11] The light and the sun rose up, and the lowly were exalted, and devoured the glorious. [12] Now when Mardocheus, who had seen this dream,

and what God had determined to do, was awake, he bare this dream in mind, and until night by all means was desirous to know it.

12 [1] And Mardocheus took his rest in the court with Gabatha and Tharra, the two eunuchs of the king, and keepers of the palace. [2] And he heard their devices, and searched out their purposes, and learned that they were about to lay hands upon Artaxerxes the king; and so he certified the king of them. [3] Then the king examined the two eunuchs, and after that they had confessed it, they were strangled. [4] And the king made a record of these things, and Mardocheus also wrote thereof. [5] So the king commanded Mardocheus to serve in the court, and for this he rewarded him. [6] Howbeit Aman the son of Amadathus the Agagite, who was in great honour with the king, sought to molest Mardocheus and his people because of the two eunuchs of the king.

13 [1] The copy of the letters was this: The great king Artaxerxes writeth these things to the princes and governors that are under him from India unto Ethiopia in an hundred and seven and twenty provinces. [2] After that I became lord over many nations and had dominion over the whole world, not lifted up with presumption of my authority, but carrying myself always with equity and mildness, I purposed to settle my subjects continually in a quiet life, and making my kingdom peaceable, and open for passage to the utmost coasts, to renew peace, which is desired of all men. [3] Now when I asked my counsellors how this might be brought to pass, Aman, that excelled in wisdom among us, and was approved for his constant good will and steadfast fidelity, and had the honour of the second place in the

kingdom, [4] declared unto us, that in all nations throughout the world there was scattered a certain malicious people, that had laws contrary to all nations, and continually despised the commandments of kings, so as the uniting of our kingdoms, honourably intended by us, cannot go forward. [5] Seeing then we understand that this people alone is continually in opposition unto all men, differing in the strange manner of their laws, and evil affected to our state, working all the mischief they can that our kingdom may not be firmly established: [6] Therefore have we commanded, that all they that are signified in writing unto you by Aman, who is ordained over the affairs, and is next unto us, shall all with their wives and children be utterly destroyed by the sword of their enemies, without all mercy and pity, the fourteenth day of the twelfth month Adar of this present year: [7] That they, who of old and now also are malicious, may in one day with violence go into the grave, and so ever hereafter cause our affairs to be well settled, and without trouble. [8] Then Mardocheus thought upon all the works of the Lord, and made his prayer unto him, [9] saying, O Lord, Lord, the King Almighty: for the whole world is in thy power, and if thou hast appointed to save Israel, there is no man that can gainsay thee: [10] For thou hast made heaven and earth, and all the wondrous things under the heaven. [11] Thou art Lord of all things, and there is no man that can resist thee, which art the Lord. [12] Thou knowest all things, and thou knowest, Lord, that it was neither in contempt nor pride, nor for any desire of glory, that I did not bow down to proud Aman. [13] For I could have been content with good will for the salvation of Israel to kiss the soles of his feet. [14] But I did this, that I might not prefer the glory of man above the glory of God: neither will I worship any but thee, O God, neither will I do it in pride. [15] And now, O Lord God and King, spare thy people: for their eyes are upon us to bring us to nought; yea, they desire to destroy the inheritance, that hath been thine from the beginning. [16] Despise not the portion which thou hast delivered out of Egypt for thine own self. [17] Hear my prayer, and be merciful unto thine inheritance: turn our sorrow into joy, that we may live, O Lord, and praise thy name: and destroy not the mouths of them that praise thee, O Lord. [18] All Israel in like manner cried most earnestly unto the Lord, because their death was before their eyes.

14 [1] Queen Esther also being in fear of death, resorted unto the Lord: [2] and laid away her glorious apparel, and put on the garments of anguish and mourning: and instead of precious ointments, she covered her head with ashes and dung, and she humbled her body greatly, and all the places of her joy she filled with her torn hair. [3] And she prayed unto the Lord God of Israel, saying, O my Lord, thou only art our King: help me, desolate woman, which have no helper but thee: [4] For my danger is in mine hand. [5] From my youth up I have heard in the tribe of my family that thou, O Lord, tookest Israel from among all people, and our fathers from all their predecessors, for a perpetual inheritance, and thou hast performed whatsoever thou didst promise them. [6] And now we have sinned before thee: therefore hast thou given us into the hands of our enemies, [7] Because we worshipped their gods: O Lord, thou art righteous. [8] Nevertheless it satisfieth them not, that we are in bitter captivity: but they have stricken hands with their idols, [9] that they will abolish the thing that

thou with thy mouth hast ordained, and destroy thine inheritance, and stop the mouth of them that praise thee, and quench the glory of thy house, and of thine altar, [10] and open the mouths of the heathen to set forth the praises of the idols, and to magnify a fleshly king for ever. [11] O Lord, give not thy sceptre unto them that be nothing, and let them not laugh at our fall; but turn their device upon themselves, and make him an example, that hath begun this against us. [12] Remember, O Lord, make thyself known in time of our affliction, and give me boldness, O King of the nations, and Lord of all power. [13] Give me eloquent speech in my mouth before the lion: turn his heart to hate him that fighteth against us, that there may be an end of him, and of all that are likeminded to him: [14] But deliver us with thine hand, and help me that am desolate, and which have no other help but thee. [15] Thou knowest all things, O Lord; thou knowest that I hate the glory of the unrighteous, and abhor the bed of the uncircumcised, and of all the heathen. [16] Thou knowest my necessity: for I abhor the sign of my high estate, which is upon mine head in the days wherein I shew myself, and that I abhor it as a menstruous rag, and that I wear it not when I am private by myself. [17] And that thine handmaid hath not eaten at Aman's table, and that I have not greatly esteemed the king's feast, nor drunk the wine of the drink offerings. [18] Neither had thine handmaid any joy since the day that I was brought hither to this present, but in thee, O Lord God of Abraham. [19] O thou mighty God above all, hear the voice of the forlorn and deliver us out of the hands of the mischievous, and deliver me out of my fear.

15 [1] And upon the third day, when she had ended her prayers, she laid away her mourning garments, and put on her glorious apparel. [2] And being gloriously adorned, after she had called upon God, who is the beholder and saviour of all things, she took two maids with her: [3] And upon the one she leaned, as carrying herself daintily; [4] and the other followed, bearing up her train. [5] And she was ruddy through the perfection of her beauty, and her countenance was cheerful and very amiable: but her heart was in anguish for fear. [6] Then having passed through all the doors, she stood before the king, who sat upon his royal throne, and was clothed with all his robes of majesty, all glittering with gold and precious stones; and he was very dreadful. [7] Then lifting up his countenance that shone with majesty, he looked very fiercely upon her: and the queen fell down, and was pale, and fainted, and bowed herself upon the head of the maid that went before her. [8] Then God changed the spirit of the king into mildness, who in a fear leaped from his throne, and took her in his arms, till she came to herself again, and comforted her with loving words and said unto her, [9] Esther, what is the matter? I am thy brother, be of good cheer: [10] Thou shalt not die, though our commandment be general: come near. [11] And so he held up his golden sceptre, and laid it upon her neck, [12] and embraced her, and said, Speak unto me. [13] Then said she unto him, I saw thee, my lord, as an angel of God, and my heart was troubled for fear of thy majesty. [14] For wonderful art thou, lord, and thy countenance is full of grace. [15] And as she was speaking, she fell down for faintness. [16] Then the king was troubled, and all his servants comforted her.

16 [1] The great king Artaxerxes unto the princes and governors of an hundred and seven and twenty provinces from India unto Ethiopia, and unto all our faithful subjects, greeting. [2] Many, the more often they are honoured with the great bounty of their gracious princes, the more proud they are waxen, [3] and endeavour to hurt not our subjects only, but not being able to bear abundance, do take in hand to practise also against those that do them good: [4] And take not only thankfulness away from among men, but also lifted up with the glorious words of lewd persons, that were never good, they think to escape the justice of God, that seeth all things and hateth evil. [5] Oftentimes also fair speech of those that are put in trust to manage their friends' affairs, hath caused many that are in authority to be partakers of innocent blood, and hath enwrapped them in remediless calamities: [6] beguiling with the falsehood and deceit of their lewd disposition the innocency and goodness of princes. [7] Now ye may see this, as we have declared, not so much by ancient histories, as ye may, if ye search what hath been wickedly done of late through the pestilent behaviour of them that are unworthily placed in authority. [8] And we must take care for the time to come, that our kingdom may be quiet and peaceable for all men, [9] both by changing our purposes, and always judging things that are evident with more equal proceeding. [10] For Aman, a Macedonian, the son of Amadatha, being indeed a stranger from the Persian blood, and far distant from our goodness, and as a stranger received of us, [11] had so far forth obtained the favour that we shew toward every nation, as that he was called our father, and was continually honoured of all men, the next person unto the king. [12] But he, not bearing his great dignity, went

about to deprive us of our kingdom and life: [13] having by manifold and cunning deceits sought of us the destruction, as well of Mardocheus, who saved our life, and continually procured our good, as also of blameless Esther, partaker of our kingdom, with their whole nation. [14] For by these means he thought, finding us destitute of friends, to have translated the kingdom of the Persians to the Macedonians. [15] But we find that the Jews, whom this wicked wretch hath delivered to utter destruction, are no evildoers, but live by most just laws: [16] And that they be children of the most high and most mighty, living God, who hath ordered the kingdom both unto us and to our progenitors in the most excellent manner. [17] Wherefore ye shall do well not to put in execution the letters sent unto you by Aman the son of Amadatha. [18] For he that was the worker of these things, is hanged at the gates of Susa with all his family: God, who ruleth all things, speedily rendering vengeance to him according to his deserts. [19] Therefore ye shall publish the copy of this letter in all places, that the Jews may freely live after their own laws. [20] And ye shall aid them, that even the same day, being the thirteenth day of the twelfth month Adar, they may be avenged on them, who in the time of their affliction shall set upon them. [21] For Almighty God hath turned to joy unto them the day, wherein the chosen people should have perished. [22] Ye shall therefore among your solemn feasts keep it an high day with all feasting: [23] that both now and hereafter there may be safety to us and the well affected Persians; but to those which do conspire against us, a memorial of destruction. [24] Therefore every city and country whatsoever, which shall not do according to these things, shall be destroyed without mercy with fire and sword, and shall be made not only unpassable for men, but also most hateful to wild beasts and fowls for ever.

THE WISDOM OF SOLOMON

1 [1] Love righteousness, ye that be judges of the earth: think of the Lord with a good (heart,) and in simplicity of heart seek him. [2] For he will be found of them that tempt him not; and sheweth himself unto such as do not distrust him. [3] For froward thoughts separate from God: and his power, when it is tried, reproveth the unwise. [4] For into a malicious soul wisdom shall not enter; nor dwell in the body that is subject unto sin. [5] For the holy spirit of discipline will flee deceit, and remove from thoughts that are without understanding, and will not abide when unrighteousness cometh in. [6] For wisdom is a loving spirit; and will not acquit a blasphemer of his words: for God is witness of his reins, and a true beholder of his heart, and a hearer of his tongue. [7] For the Spirit of the Lord filleth the world: and that which containeth all things hath knowledge of the voice. [8] Therefore he that speaketh unrighteous things cannot be hid: neither shall vengeance, when it punisheth, pass by him. [9] For inquisition shall be made into the counsels of the ungodly: and the sound of his words shall come unto the Lord for the manifestation

of his wicked deeds. [10] For the ear of jealousy heareth all things: and the noise of murmurings is not hid. [11] Therefore beware of murmuring, which is unprofitable; and refrain your tongue from backbiting: for there is no word so secret, that shall go for nought: and the mouth that belieth slayeth the soul. [12] Seek not death in the error of your life: and pull not upon yourselves destruction with the works of your hands. [13] For God made not death: neither hath he pleasure in the destruction of the living. [14] For he created all things, that they might have their being: and the generations of the world were healthful; and there is no poison of destruction in them, nor the kingdom of death upon the earth: [15] (For righteousness is immortal.) [16] But ungodly men with their works and words called it to them: for when they thought to have it their friend, they consumed to nought, and made a covenant with it, because they are worthy to take part with it.

2 [1] For the ungodly said, reasoning with themselves, but not aright, Our life is short and tedious, and in the death of a man there is no remedy: neither was there any man known to have returned from the grave. [2] For we are born at all adventure: and we shall be hereafter as though we had never been: for the breath in our nostrils is as smoke, and a little spark in the moving of our heart: [3] which being extinguished, our body shall be turned into ashes, and our spirit shall vanish as the soft air, [4] and our name shall be forgotten in time, and no man shall have our works in remembrance, and our life shall pass away as the trace of a cloud, and shall be dispersed as a mist that is driven away with the beams of the sun, and overcome with the heat thereof. [5] For our time is a very shadow that passeth away; and after our

end there is no returning: for it is fast sealed, so that no man cometh again. [6] Come on therefore, let us enjoy the good things that are present: and let us speedily use the creatures like as in youth. [7] Let us fill ourselves with costly wine and ointments: and let no flower of the spring pass by us. [8] Let us crown ourselves with rose-buds, before they be withered. [9] Let none of us go without his part of our voluptuousness: let us leave tokens of our joyfulness in every place: for this is our portion, and our lot is this. [10] Let us oppress the poor righteous man, let us not spare the widow, nor reverence the ancient gray hairs of the aged. [11] Let our strength be the law of justice: for that which is feeble is found to be nothing worth. [12] Therefore let us lie in wait for the righteous; because he is not for our turn, and he is clean contrary to our doings: he upbraideth us with our offending the law, and objecteth to our infamy the transgressings of our education. [13] He professeth to have the knowledge of God; and he calleth himself the child of the Lord. [14] He was made to reprove our thoughts. [15] He is grievous unto us even to behold: for his life is not like other men's, his ways are of another fashion. [16] We are esteemed of him as counterfeits: he abstaineth from our ways as from filthiness: he pronounceth the end of the just to be blessed, and maketh his boast that God is his father. [17] Let us see if his words be true: and let us prove what shall happen in the end of him. [18] For if the just man be the son of God, he will help him, and deliver him from the hand of his enemies. [19] Let us examine him with despitefulness and torture, that we may know his meekness, and prove his patience. [20] Let us condemn him with a shameful death: for by his own saying he shall be respected. [21] Such things they did imagine, and were deceived: for their own wickedness hath blinded them. [22] As for the mysteries of God, they knew them not: neither hoped they for the wages of righteousness, nor discerned a reward for blameless souls. [23] For God created man to be immortal, and made him to be an image of his own eternity. [24] Nevertheless through envy of the devil came death into the world: and they that do hold of his side do find it.

3 [1] But the souls of the righteous are in the hand of God, and there shall no torment touch them. [2] In the sight of the unwise they seemed to die: and their departure is taken for misery, [3] and their going from us to be utter destruction: but they are in peace. [4] For though they be punished in the sight of men, yet is their hope full of immortality. [5] And having been a little chastised, they shall be greatly rewarded: for God proved them, and found them worthy for himself. [6] As gold in the furnace hath he tried them, and received them as a burnt offering. [7] And in the time of their visitation they shall shine, and run to and fro like sparks among the stubble. [8] They shall judge the nations, and have dominion over the people, and their Lord shall reign for ever. [9] They that put their trust in him shall understand the truth: and such as be faithful in love shall abide with him: for grace and mercy is to his saints, and he hath care for his elect. [10] But the ungodly shall be punished according to their own imaginations, which have neglected the righteous, and forsaken the Lord. [11] For whoso despiseth wisdom and nurture, he is miserable, and their hope is vain, their labours unfruitful, and their works unprofitable: [12] Their wives are foolish, and their children wicked: [13] Their offspring is cursed. Wherefore blessed is the barren that is undefiled, which hath not

known the sinful bed: she shall have fruit in the visitation of souls. [14] And blessed is the eunuch, which with his hands hath wrought no iniquity, nor imagined wicked things against God: for unto him shall be given the special gift of faith, and an inheritance in the temple of the Lord more acceptable to his mind. [15] For glorious is the fruit of good labours: and the root of wisdom shall never fall away. [16] As for the children of adulterers, they shall not come to their perfection, and the seed of an unrighteous bed shall be rooted out. [17] For though they live long, yet shall they be nothing regarded: and their last age shall be without honour. [18] Or, if they die quickly, they have no hope, neither comfort in the day of trial. [19] For horrible is the end of the unrighteous generation.

4 [1] Better it is to have no children, and to have virtue: for the memorial thereof is immortal: because it is known with God, and with men. [2] When it is present, men take example at it; and when it is gone, they desire it: it weareth a crown, and triumpheth for ever, having gotten the victory, striving for undefiled rewards. [3] But the multiplying brood of the ungodly shall not thrive, nor take deep rooting from bastard slips, nor lay any fast foundation. [4] For though they flourish in branches for a time; yet standing not fast, they shall be shaken with the wind, and through the force of winds they shall be rooted out. [5] The imperfect branches shall be broken off, their fruit unprofitable, not ripe to eat, yea, meet for nothing. [6] For children begotten of unlawful beds are witnesses of wickedness against their parents in their trial. [7] But though the righteous be prevented with death, yet shall he be in rest. [8] For honourable age is not that which standeth in length of time, nor that

is measured by number of years. [9] But wisdom is the gray hair unto men, and an unspotted life is old age. [10] He pleased God, and was beloved of him: so that living among sinners he was translated. [11] Yea speedily was he taken away, lest that wickedness should alter his understanding, or deceit beguile his soul. [12] For the bewitching of naughtiness doth obscure things that are honest; and the wandering of concupiscence doth undermine the simple mind. [13] He, being made perfect in a short time, fulfilled a long time: [14] For his soul pleased the Lord: therefore hasted he to take him away from among the wicked. [15] This the people saw, and understood it not, neither laid they up this in their minds, That his grace and mercy is with his saints, and that he hath respect unto his chosen. [16] Thus the righteous that is dead shall condemn the ungodly which are living; and youth that is soon perfected the many years and old age of the unrighteous. [17] For they shall see the end of the wise, and shall not understand what God in his counsel hath decreed of him, and to what end the Lord hath set him in safety. [18] They shall see him, and despise him; but God shall laugh them to scorn: and they shall hereafter be a vile carcass, and a reproach among the dead for evermore. [19] For he shall rend them, and cast them down headlong, that they shall be speechless; and he shall shake them from the foundation; and they shall be utterly laid waste, and be in sorrow; and their memorial shall perish. [20] And when they cast up the accounts of their sins, they shall come with fear: and their own iniquities shall convince them to their face.

5 [1] Then shall the righteous man stand in great boldness before the face of such as have afflicted him, and made

no account of his labours. [2] When they see it, they shall be troubled with terrible fear, and shall be amazed at the strangeness of his salvation, so far beyond all that they looked for. [3] And they repenting and groaning for anguish of spirit shall say within themselves, This was he, whom we had sometimes in derision, and a proverb of reproach: [4] We fools accounted his life madness, and his end to be without honour: [5] How is he numbered among the children of God, and his lot is among the saints! [6] Therefore have we erred from the way of truth, and the light of righteousness hath not shined unto us, and the sun of righteousness rose not upon us. [7] We wearied ourselves in the way of wickedness and destruction: yea, we have gone through deserts, where there lay no way: but as for the way of the Lord, we have not known it. [8] What hath pride profited us? or what good hath riches with our vaunting brought us? [9] All those things are passed away like a shadow, and as a post that hasted by; [10] and as a ship that passeth over the waves of the water, which when it is gone by, the trace thereof cannot be found, neither the pathway of the keel in the waves; [11] or as when a bird hath flown through the air, there is no token of her way to be found, but the light air being beaten with the stroke of her wings and parted with the violent noise and motion of them, is passed through, and therein afterwards no sign where she went is to be found; [12] or like as when an arrow is shot at a mark, it parteth the air, which immediately cometh together again, so that a man cannot know where it went through: [13] Even so we in like manner, as soon as we were born, began to draw to our end, and had no sign of virtue to shew; but were consumed in our own wickedness. [14] For the hope of the ungodly is like dust that is blown away with the wind; like a thin froth that is driven away with the storm; like as the smoke which is dispersed here and there with a tempest, and passeth away as the remembrance of a guest that tarrieth but a day. [15] But the righteous live for evermore; their reward also is with the Lord, and the care of them is with the most High. [16] Therefore shall they receive a glorious kingdom, and a beautiful crown from the Lord's hand: for with his right hand shall he cover them, and with his arm shall he protect them. [17] He shall take to him his jealousy for complete armour, and make the creature his weapon for the revenge of his enemies. [18] He shall put on righteousness as a breastplate, and true judgment instead of an helmet. [19] He shall take holiness for an invincible shield. [20] His severe wrath shall he sharpen for a sword, and the world shall fight with him against the unwise. [21] Then shall the right aiming thunderbolts go abroad; and from the clouds, as from a well drawn bow, shall they fly to the mark. [22] And hailstones full of wrath shall be cast as out of a stone bow, and the water of the sea shall rage against them, and the floods shall cruelly drown them. [23] Yea, a mighty wind shall stand up against them, and like a storm shall blow them away: thus iniquity shall lay waste the whole earth, and ill dealing shall overthrow the thrones of the mighty.

6 [1] Hear therefore, O ye kings, and understand; learn, ye that be judges of the ends of the earth. [2] Give ear, ye that rule the people, and glory in the multitude of nations. [3] For power is given you of the Lord, and sovereignty from the Highest, who shall try your works, and search out your counsels. [4] Because, being ministers of his kingdom, ye have not judged aright, nor kept

the law, nor walked after the counsel of God; [5] horribly and speedily shall he come upon you: for a sharp judgment shall be to them that be in high places. [6] For mercy will soon pardon the meanest: but mighty men shall be mightily tormented. [7] For he which is Lord over all shall fear no man's person, neither shall he stand in awe of any man's greatness: for he hath made the small and great, and careth for all alike. [8] But a sore trial shall come upon the mighty. [9] Unto you therefore, O kings, do I speak, that ye may learn wisdom, and not fall away. [10] For they that keep holiness holily shall be judged holy: and they that have learned such things shall find what to answer. [11] Wherefore set your affection upon my words; desire them, and ye shall be instructed. [12] Wisdom is glorious, and never fadeth away: yea, she is easily seen of them that love her, and found of such as seek her. [13] She preventeth them that desire her, in making herself first known unto them. [14] Whoso seeketh her early shall have no great travail: for he shall find her sitting at his doors. [15] To think therefore upon her is perfection of wisdom: and whoso watcheth for her shall quickly be without care. [16] For she goeth about seeking such as are worthy of her, sheweth herself favourably unto them in the ways, and meeteth them in every thought. [17] For the very true beginning of her is the desire of discipline; and the care of discipline is love; [18] and love is the keeping of her laws; and the giving heed unto her laws is the assurance of incorruption; [19] and incorruption maketh us near unto God: [20] Therefore the desire of wisdom bringeth to a kingdom. [21] If your delight be then in thrones and sceptres, O ye kings of the people, honour wisdom, that ye may reign for evermore. [22] As for wisdom, what she is, and how she came up, I will tell you, and will not hide mysteries from you: but will seek her out from the beginning of her nativity, and bring the knowledge of her into light, and will not pass over the truth. [23] Neither will I go with consuming envy; for such a man shall have no fellowship with wisdom. [24] But the multitude of the wise is the welfare of the world: and a wise king is the upholding of the people. [25] Receive therefore instruction through my words, and it shall do you good.

7 [1] I myself also am a mortal man, like to all, and the offspring of him that was first made of the earth; [2] and in my mother's womb was fashioned to be flesh in the time of ten months, being compacted in blood, of the seed of man, and the pleasure that came with sleep. [3] And when I was born, I drew in the common air, and fell upon the earth, which is of like nature, and the first voice which I uttered was crying, as all others do. [4] I was nursed in swaddling clothes, and that with cares. [5] For there is no king that had any other beginning of birth. [6] For all men have one entrance into life, and the like going out. [7] Wherefore I prayed, and understanding was given me: I called upon God, and the spirit of wisdom came to me. [8] I preferred her before sceptres and thrones, and esteemed riches nothing in comparison of her. [9] Neither compared I unto her any precious stone, because all gold in respect of her is as a little sand, and silver shall be counted as clay before her. [10] I loved her above health and beauty, and chose to have her instead of light: for the light that cometh from her never goeth out. [11] All good things together came to me with her, and innumerable riches in her hands. [12] And I rejoiced in them all, because wisdom goeth before them: and I knew not that she was the mother

of them. [13] I learned diligently, and do communicate her liberally: I do not hide her riches. [14] For she is a treasure unto men that never faileth: which they that use become the friends of God, being commended for the gifts that come from learning. [15] God hath granted me to speak as I would, and to conceive as is meet for the things that are given me: because it is he that leadeth unto wisdom, and directeth the wise. [16] For in his hand are both we and our words; all wisdom also, and knowledge of workmanship. [17] For he hath given me certain knowledge of the things that are, namely, to know how the world was made, and the operation of the elements: [18] the beginning, ending, and midst of the times: the alterations of the turning of the sun, and the change of seasons: [19] the circuits of years, and the positions of stars: [20] the natures of living creatures, and the furies of wild beasts: the violence of winds, and the reasonings of men: the diversities of plants and the virtues of roots: [21] And all such things as are either secret or manifest, them I know. [22] For wisdom, which is the worker of all things, taught me: for in her is an understanding spirit, holy, one only, manifold, subtil, lively, clear, undefiled, plain, not subject to hurt, loving the thing that is good, quick, which cannot be letted, ready to do good, [23] kind to man, steadfast, sure, free from care, having all power, overseeing all things, and going through all understanding, pure, and most subtil, spirits. [24] For wisdom is more moving than any motion: she passeth and goeth through all things by reason of her pureness. [25] For she is the breath of the power of God, and a pure influence flowing from the glory of the Almighty: therefore can no defiled thing fall into her. [26] For she is the brightness of the everlasting light, the unspotted mirror of the power of God, and the image of his goodness. [27] And being but one, she can do all things: and remaining in herself, she maketh all things new: and in all ages entering into holy souls, she maketh them friends of God, and prophets. [28] For God loveth none but him that dwelleth with wisdom. [29] For she is more beautiful than the sun, and above all the order of stars: being compared with the light, she is found before it. [30] For after this cometh night: but vice shall not prevail against wisdom.

8 [1] Wisdom reacheth from one end to another mightily: and sweetly doth she order all things. [2] I loved her, and sought her out from my youth, I desired to make her my spouse, and I was a lover of her beauty. [3] In that she is conversant with God, she magnifieth her nobility: yea, the Lord of all things himself loved her. [4] For she is privy to the mysteries of the knowledge of God, and a lover of his works. [5] If riches be a possession to be desired in this life; what is richer than wisdom, that worketh all things? [6] And if prudence work; who of all that are is a more cunning workman than she? [7] And if a man love righteousness, her labours are virtues: for she teacheth temperance and prudence, justice and fortitude: which are such things as men can have nothing more profitable in their life. [8] If a man desire much experience, she knoweth things of old, and conjectureth aright what is to come: she knoweth the subtilties of speeches, and can expound dark sentences: she foreseeth signs and wonders, and the events of seasons and times. [9] Therefore I purposed to take her to me to live with me, knowing that she would be a counsellor of good things, and a comfort in cares and grief. [10] For her sake I shall have estimation among the multitude, and honour with the elders, though I be young. [11] I

shall be found of a quick conceit in judgment, and shall be admired in the sight of great men. [12] When I hold my tongue, they shall abide my leisure, and when I speak, they shall give good ear unto me: if I talk much, they shall lay their hands upon their mouth. [13] Moreover by the means of her I shall obtain immortality, and leave behind me an everlasting memorial to them that come after me. [14] I shall set the people in order, and the nations shall be subject unto me. [15] Horrible tyrants shall be afraid when they do but hear of me; I shall be found good among the multitude, and valiant in war. [16] After I am come into mine house, I will repose myself with her: for her conversation hath no bitterness; and to live with her hath no sorrow, but mirth and joy. [17] Now when I considered these things in myself, and pondered them in my heart, how that to be allied unto wisdom is immortality; [18] and great pleasure it is to have her friendship; and in the works of her hands are infinite riches; and in the exercise of conference with her, prudence; and in talking with her, a good report; I went about seeking how to take her to me. [19] For I was a witty child, and had a good spirit. [20] Yea rather, being good, I came into a body undefiled. [21] Nevertheless, when I perceived that I could not otherwise obtain her, except God gave her me; and that was a point of wisdom also to know whose gift she was; I prayed unto the Lord, and besought him, and with my whole heart I said,

9 [1] O God of my fathers, and Lord of mercy, who hast made all things with thy word, [2] and ordained man through thy wisdom, that he should have dominion over the creatures which thou hast made, [3] and order the world according to equity and righteousness, and

execute judgment with an upright heart: [4] Give me wisdom, that sitteth by thy throne; and reject me not from among thy children: [5] For I thy servant and son of thine handmaid am a feeble person, and of a short time, and too young for the understanding of judgment and laws. [6] For though a man be never so perfect among the children of men, yet if thy wisdom be not with him, he shall be nothing regarded. [7] Thou hast chosen me to be a king of thy people, and a judge of thy sons and daughters: [8] Thou hast commanded me to build a temple upon thy holy mount, and an altar in the city wherein thou dwellest, a resemblance of the holy tabernacle, which thou hast prepared from the beginning. [9] And wisdom was with thee: which knoweth thy works, and was present when thou madest the world, and knew what was acceptable in thy sight, and right in thy commandments. [10] O send her out of thy holy heavens, and from the throne of thy glory, that being present she may labour with me, that I may know what is pleasing unto thee. [11] For she knoweth and understandeth all things, and she shall lead me soberly in my doings, and preserve me in her power. [12] So shall my works be acceptable, and then shall I judge thy people righteously, and be worthy to sit in my father's seat. [13] For what man is he that can know the counsel of God? or who can think what the will of the Lord is? [14] For the thoughts of mortal men are miserable, and our devices are but uncertain. [15] For the corruptible body presseth down the soul, and the earthly tabernacle weigheth down the mind that museth upon many things. [16] And hardly do we guess aright at things that are upon earth, and with labour do we find the things that are before us: but the things that are in heaven who hath searched out? [17] And thy counsel who hath known, except thou give wisdom, and send thy Holy Spirit from above? [18] For so the ways of them which lived on the earth were reformed, and men were taught the things that are pleasing unto thee, and were saved through wisdom.

10 [1] She preserved the first formed father of the world, that was created alone, and brought him out of his fall, [2] and gave him power to rule all things. [3] But when the unrighteous went away from her in his anger, he perished also in the fury wherewith he murdered his brother. [4] For whose cause the earth being drowned with the flood, wisdom again preserved it, and directed the course of the righteous in a piece of wood of small value. [5] Moreover, the nations in their wicked conspiracy being confounded, she found out the righteous, and preserved him blameless unto God, and kept him strong against his tender compassion toward his son. [6] When the ungodly perished, she delivered the righteous man, who fled from the fire which fell down upon the five cities. [7] Of whose wickedness even to this day the waste land that smoketh is a testimony, and plants bearing fruit that never come to ripeness: and a standing pillar of salt is a monument of an unbelieving soul. [8] For regarding not wisdom, they gat not only this hurt, that they knew not the things which were good; but also left behind them to the world a memorial of their foolishness: so that in the things wherein they offended they could not so much as be hid. [9] But wisdom delivered from pain those that attended upon her. [10] When the righteous fled from his brother's wrath, she guided him in right paths, shewed him the kingdom of God, and gave him knowledge of holy things, made him rich in his travels, and multiplied the fruit of his labours. [11] In the covetousness of such as oppressed him

she stood by him, and made him rich. [12] She defended him from his enemies, and kept him safe from those that lay in wait, and in a sore conflict she gave him the victory; that he might know that goodness is stronger than all. [13] When the righteous was sold, she forsook him not, but delivered him from sin: she went down with him into the pit, [14] and left him not in bonds, till she brought him the sceptre of the kingdom, and power against those that oppressed him: as for them that had accused him, she shewed them to be liars, and gave him perpetual glory. [15] She delivered the righteous people and blameless seed from the nation that oppressed them. [16] She entered into the soul of the servant of the Lord, and withstood dreadful kings in wonders and signs; [17] rendered to the righteous a reward of their labours, guided them in a marvellous way, and was unto them for a cover by day, and a light of stars in the night season; [18] brought them through the Red Sea, and led them through much water: [19] But she drowned their enemies, and cast them up out of the bottom of the deep. [20] Therefore the righteous spoiled the ungodly, and praised thy holy name, O Lord, and magnified with one accord thine hand that fought for them. [21] For wisdom opened the mouth of the dumb, and made the tongues of them that cannot speak eloquent.

11 [1] She prospered their works in the hand of the holy prophet. [2] They went through the wilderness that was not inhabited, and pitched tents in places where there lay no way. [3] They stood against their enemies, and were avenged of their adversaries. [4] When they were thirsty, they called upon thee, and water was given them out of the flinty rock, and their thirst was quenched out of the hard stone. [5] For by what things

their enemies were punished, by the same they in their need were benefited. [6] For instead of a perpetual running river troubled with foul blood, [7] for a manifest reproof of that commandment, whereby the infants were slain, thou gavest unto them abundance of water by a means which they hoped not for: [8] Declaring by that thirst then how thou hadst punished their adversaries. [9] For when they were tried albeit but in mercy chastised, they knew how the ungodly were judged in wrath and tormented, thirsting in another manner than the just. [10] For these thou didst admonish and try, as a father: but the other, as a severe king, thou didst condemn and punish. [11] Whether they were absent or present, they were vexed alike. [12] For a double grief came upon them, and a groaning for the remembrance of things past. [13] For when they heard by their own punishments the other to be benefited, they had some feeling of the Lord. [14] For whom they rejected with scorn, when he was long before thrown out at the casting forth of the infants, him in the end, when they saw what came to pass, they admired. [15] But for the foolish devices of their wickedness, wherewith being deceived they worshipped serpents void of reason, and vile beasts, thou didst send a multitude of unreasonable beasts upon them for vengeance; [16] that they might know, that wherewithal a man sinneth, by the same also shall he be punished. [17] For thine Almighty hand, that made the world of matter without form, wanted not means to send among them a multitude of bears, or fierce lions, [18] or unknown wild beasts, full of rage, newly created, breathing out either a fiery vapour, or filthy scents of scattered smoke, or shooting horrible sparkles out of their eyes: [19] Whereof not only the harm might dispatch them at once, but also the terrible sight utterly destroy them. [20] Yea, and without these might they have fallen down with one blast, being persecuted of vengeance, and scattered abroad through the breath of thy power: but thou hast ordered all things in measure and number and weight. [21] For thou canst shew thy great strength at all times when thou wilt; and who may withstand the power of thine arm? [22] For the whole world before thee is as a little grain of the balance, yea, as a drop of the morning dew that falleth down upon the earth. [23] But thou hast mercy upon all; for thou canst do all things, and winkest at the sins of men, because they should amend. [24] For thou lovest all the things that are, and abhorrest nothing which thou hast made: for never wouldest thou have made any thing, if thou hadst hated it. [25] And how could any thing have endured, if it had not been thy will? or been preserved, if not called by thee? [26] But thou sparest all: for they are thine, O Lord, thou lover of souls.

12 [1] For thine incorruptible Spirit is in all things. [2] Therefore chastenest thou them by little and little that offend, and warnest them by putting them in remembrance wherein they have offended, that leaving their wickedness they may believe on thee, O Lord. [3] For it was thy will to destroy by the hands of our fathers both those old inhabitants of thy holy land, [4] whom thou hatedst for doing most odious works of witchcrafts, and wicked sacrifices; [5] and also those merciless murderers of children, and devourers of man's flesh, and the feasts of blood, [6] with their priests out of the midst of their idolatrous crew, and the parents that killed with their own hands souls destitute of help: [7] That the land, which thou esteemedst above all other, might receive a worthy colony of God's children. [8] Nevertheless, even

those thou sparedst as men, and didst send wasps, forerunners of thine host, to destroy them by little and little. [9] Not that thou wast unable to bring the ungodly under the hand of the righteous in battle, or to destroy them at once with cruel beasts, or with one rough word: [10] but executing thy judgments upon them by little and little, thou gavest them place of repentance, not being ignorant that they were a naughty generation, and that their malice was bred in them, and that their cogitation would never be changed. [11] For it was a cursed seed from the beginning; neither didst thou for fear of any man give them pardon for those things wherein they sinned. [12] For who shall say, What hast thou done? or who shall withstand thy judgment? or who shall accuse thee for the nations that perish, whom thou made? or who shall come to stand against thee, to be revenged for the unrighteous men? [13] For neither is there any God but thou that careth for all, to whom thou mightest shew that thy judgment is not unright. [14] Neither shall king or tyrant be able to set his face against thee for any whom thou hast punished. [15] Forsomuch then as thou art righteous thyself, thou orderest all things righteously: thinking it not agreeable with thy power to condemn him that hath not deserved to be punished. [16] For thy power is the beginning of righteousness, and because thou art the Lord of all, it maketh thee to be gracious unto all. [17] For when men will not believe that thou art of a full power, thou shewest thy strength, and among them that know it thou makest their boldness manifest. [18] But thou, mastering thy power, judgest with equity, and orderest us with great favour: for thou mayest use power when thou wilt. [19] But by such works hast thou taught thy people that the just man should be merciful, and hast made thy children to be of a good hope that thou givest repentance for sins. [20] For if thou didst punish the enemies of thy children, and the condemned to death, with such deliberation, giving them time and place, whereby they might be delivered from their malice: [21] with how great circumspection didst thou judge thine own sons, unto whose fathers thou hast sworn, and made covenants of good promises? [22] Therefore, whereas thou dost chasten us, thou scourgest our enemies a thousand times more, to the intent that, when we judge, we should carefully think of thy goodness, and when we ourselves are judged, we should look for mercy. [23] Wherefore, whereas men have lived dissolutely and unrighteously, thou hast tormented them with their own abominations. [24] For they went astray very far in the ways of error, and held them for gods, which even among the beasts of their enemies were despised, being deceived, as children of no understanding. [25] Therefore unto them, as to children without the use of reason, thou didst send a judgment to mock them. [26] But they that would not be reformed by that correction, wherein he dallied with them, shall feel a judgment worthy of God. [27] For, look, for what things they grudged, when they were punished, that is, for them whom they thought to be gods; [now] being punished in them, when they saw it, they acknowledged him to be the true God, whom before they denied to know: and therefore came extreme damnation upon them.

13 [1] Surely vain are all men by nature, who are ignorant of God, and could not out of the good things that are seen know him that is: neither, by considering the works, did they acknowledge the workmaster; [2] but deemed either fire, or wind, or the swift air, or the circle of the

stars, or the violent water, or the lights of heaven, to be the gods which govern the world. [3] With whose beauty if they being delighted took them to be gods; let them know how much better the Lord of them is: for the first author of beauty hath created them. [4] But if they were astonished at their power and virtue, let them understand by them, how much mightier he is that made them. [5] For by the greatness and beauty of the creatures proportionably the maker of them is seen. [6] But yet for this they are the less to be blamed: for they peradventure err, seeking God, and desirous to find him. [7] For being conversant in his works, they search him diligently, and believe their sight: because the things are beautiful that are seen. [8] Howbeit, neither are they to be pardoned. [9] For if they were able to know so much, that they could aim at the world; how did they not sooner find out the Lord thereof? [10] But miserable are they, and in dead things is their hope, who call them gods, which are the works of men's hands, gold and silver, to shew art in, and resemblances of beasts, or a stone good for nothing, the work of an ancient hand. [11] Now a carpenter that felleth timber, after he hath sawn down a tree meet for the purpose, and taken off all the bark skilfully round about, and hath wrought it handsomely, and made a vessel thereof fit for the service of man's life; [12] and after spending the refuse of his work to dress his meat, hath filled himself; [13] and taking the very refuse among those which served to no use, being a crooked piece of wood, and full of knots, hath carved it diligently, when he had nothing else to do, and formed it by the skill of his understanding, and fashioned it to the image of a man; [14] or made it like some vile beast, laying it over with vermilion, and with paint colouring it red, and covering every spot therein;

[15] and when he had made a convenient room for it, set it in a wall, and made it fast with iron: [16] For he provided for it that it might not fall, knowing that it was unable to help itself; for it is an image, and hath need of help: [17] Then maketh he prayer for his goods, for his wife and children, and is not ashamed to speak to that which hath no life. [18] For health, he calleth upon that which is weak: for life, prayeth to that which is dead; for aid, humbly beseecheth that which hath least means to help: and for a good journey, he asketh of that which cannot set a foot forward: [19] And for gaining and getting, and for good success of his hands, asketh ability to do, of him that is most unable to do any thing.

14 [1] Again, one preparing himself to sail, and about to pass through the raging waves, calleth upon a piece of wood more rotten than the vessel that carrieth him. [2] For verily desire of gain devised that, and the workman built it by his skill. [3] But thy providence, O Father, governeth it: for thou hast made a way in the sea, and a safe path in the waves; [4] shewing that thou canst save from all danger: yea, though a man went to sea without art. [5] Nevertheless thou wouldest not that the works of thy wisdom should be idle, and therefore do men commit their lives to a small piece of wood, and passing the rough sea in a weak vessel are saved. [6] For in the old time also, when the proud giants perished, the hope of the world, governed by thy hand, escaped in a weak vessel, and left to all ages a seed of generation. [7] For blessed is the wood whereby righteousness cometh. [8] But that which is made with hands is cursed, as well it, as he that made it: he, because he made it; and it, because being corruptible, it was called God. [9] For the ungodly and his ungodliness are both alike hateful unto

God. [10] For that which is made shall be punished together with him that made it. [11] Therefore even upon the idols of the Gentiles shall there be a visitation: because in the creature of God they are become an abomination, and stumbling blocks to the souls of men, and a snare to the feet of the unwise. [12] For the devising of idols was the beginning of spiritual fornication, and the invention of them the corruption of life. [13] For neither were they from the beginning, neither shall they be for ever. [14] For by the vain glory of men they entered into the world, and therefore shall they come shortly to an end. [15] For a father afflicted with untimely mourning, when he hath made an image of his child soon taken away, now honoured him as a god, which was then a dead man, and delivered to those that were under him ceremonies and sacrifices. [16] Thus in process of time an ungodly custom grown strong was kept as a law, and graven images were worshipped by the commandments of kings. [17] Whom men could not honour in presence, because they dwelt far off, they took the counterfeit of his visage from far, and made an express image of a king whom they honoured, to the end that by this their forwardness they might flatter him that was absent, as if he were present. [18] Also the singular diligence of the artificer did help to set forward the ignorant to more superstition. [19] For he, peradventure willing to please one in authority, forced all his skill to make the resemblance of the best fashion. [20] And so the multitude, allured by the grace of the work, took him now for a god, which a little before was but honoured as a man. [21] And this was an occasion to deceive the world: for men, serving either calamity or tyranny, did ascribe unto stones and stocks the incommunicable name. [22] Moreover, this was not enough for them, that they erred in the knowledge of God; but whereas they lived in the great war of ignorance, those so great plagues called they peace. [23] For whilst they slew their children in sacrifices, or used secret ceremonies, or made revellings of strange rites; [24] they kept neither lives nor marriages any longer undefiled: but either one slew another traitorously, or grieved him by adultery. [25] So that there reigned in all men without exception, blood, manslaughter, theft, and dissimulation, corruption, unfaithfulness, tumults, perjury, [26] disquieting of good men, forgetfulness of good turns, defiling of souls, changing of kind, disorder in marriages, adultery, and shameless uncleanness. [27] For the worshipping of idols not to be named is the beginning, the cause, and the end, of all evil. [28] For either they are mad when they be merry, or prophesy lies, or live unjustly, or else lightly forswear themselves. [29] For insomuch as their trust is in idols which have no life; though they swear falsely, yet they look not to be hurt. [30] Howbeit, for both causes shall they be justly punished: both because they thought not well of God, giving heed unto idols, and also unjustly swore in deceit, despising holiness. [31] For it is not the power of them by whom they swear: but it is the just vengeance of sinners, that punisheth always the offence of the ungodly.

15 [1] But thou, O God, art gracious and true, longsuffering, and in mercy ordering all things. [2] For if we sin, we are thine, knowing thy power: but we will not sin, knowing that we are counted thine. [3] For to know thee is perfect righteousness: yea, to know thy power is the root of immortality. [4] For neither did the mischievous invention of men deceive us, nor an image spotted with divers colours, the painter's fruitless labour; [5] The sight

whereof enticeth fools to lust after it, and so they desire the form of a dead image, that hath no breath. [6] Both they that make them, they that desire them, and they that worship them, are lovers of evil things, and are worthy to have such things to trust upon. [7] For the potter, tempering soft earth, fashioneth every vessel with much labour for our service: yea, of the same clay he maketh both the vessels that serve for clean uses, and likewise also all such as serve to the contrary: but what is the use of either sort, the potter himself is the judge. [8] And employing his labours lewdly, he maketh a vain god of the same clay, even he which a little before was made of earth himself, and within a little while after returneth to the same out of the which he was taken, when his life which was lent him shall be demanded. [9] Notwithstanding his care is, not that he shall have much labour, nor that his life is short: but striveth to excel goldsmiths and silversmiths, and endeavoureth to do like the workers in brass, and counteth it his glory to make counterfeit things. [10] His heart is ashes, his hope is more vile than earth, and his life of less value than clay: [11] Forasmuch as he knew not his Maker, and him that inspired into him an active soul, and breathed in a living spirit. [12] But they counted our life a pastime, and our time here a market for gain: for, say they, we must be getting every way, though it be by evil means. [13] For this man, that of earthly matter maketh brittle vessels and graven images, knoweth himself to offend above all others. [14] And all the enemies of thy people, that hold them in subjection, are most foolish, and are more miserable than very babes. [15] For they counted all the idols of the heathen to be gods: which neither have the use of eyes to see, nor noses to draw breath, nor ears to hear, nor fingers of hands to handle; and as for their feet, they are slow to go. [16] For man made them, and he that borrowed his own spirit fashioned them: but no man can make a god like unto himself. [17] For being mortal, he worketh a dead thing with wicked hands: for he himself is better than the things which he worshippeth: whereas he lived once, but they never. [18] Yea, they worshipped those beasts also that are most hateful: for being compared together, some are worse than others. [19] Neither are they beautiful, so much as to be desired in respect of beasts: but they went without the praise of God and his blessing.

16 [1] Therefore by the like were they punished worthily, and by the multitude of beasts tormented. [2] Instead of which punishment, dealing graciously with thine own people, thou preparedst for them meat of a strange taste, even quails to stir up their appetite: [3] to the end that they, desiring food, might, for the ugly sight of the beasts sent among them, loathe even that which they must needs desire; but these, suffering penury for a short space, might be made partakers of a strange taste. [4] For it was requisite, that upon them exercising tyranny should come penury, which they could not avoid: but to these it should only be shewed how their enemies were tormented. [5] For when the horrible fierceness of beasts came upon these, and they perished with the stings of crooked serpents, thy wrath endured not for ever: [6] But they were troubled for a small season, that they might be admonished, having a sign of salvation, to put them in remembrance of the commandment of thy law. [7] For he that turned himself toward it was not saved by the thing that he saw, but by thee, that art the Saviour of all. [8] And in this thou madest thine enemies confess, that it is thou who deliverest from all evil; [9] for

them the bitings of grasshoppers and flies killed, neither was there found any remedy for their life: for they were worthy to be punished by such. [10] But thy sons not the very teeth of venomous dragons overcame: for thy mercy was ever by them, and healed them. [11] For they were pricked, that they should remember thy words; and were quickly saved, that not falling into deep forgetfulness, they might be continually mindful of thy goodness. [12] For it was neither herb, nor mollifying plaster, that restored them to health: but thy word, O Lord, which healeth all things. [13] For thou hast power of life and death: thou leadest to the gates of hell, and bringest up again. [14] A man indeed killeth through his malice: and the spirit, when it is gone forth, returneth not; neither the soul received up cometh again. [15] But it is not possible to escape thine hand. [16] For the ungodly, that denied to know thee, were scourged by the strength of thine arm: with strange rains, hails, and showers, were they persecuted, that they could not avoid, and through fire were they consumed. [17] For, which is most to be wondered at, the fire had more force in the water, that quencheth all things: for the world fighteth for the righteous. [18] For sometime the flame was mitigated, that it might not burn up the beasts that were sent against the ungodly; but themselves might see and perceive that they were persecuted with the judgment of God. [19] And at another time it burneth even in the midst of water above the power of fire, that it might destroy the fruits of an unjust land. [20] Instead whereof thou feddest thine own people with angels' food, and didst send them from heaven bread prepared without their labour, able to content every man's delight, and agreeing to every taste. [21] For thy sustenance declared thy sweetness unto thy children, and serving to the appetite of the eater, tempered itself to every man's liking. [22] But snow and ice endured the fire, and melted not, that they might know that fire burning in the hail, and sparkling in the rain, did destroy the fruits of the enemies. [23] But this again did even forget his own strength, that the righteous might be nourished. [24] For the creature that serveth thee, who art the Maker, increaseth his strength against the unrighteous for their punishment, and abateth his strength for the benefit of such as put their trust in thee. [25] Therefore even then was it altered into all fashions, and was obedient to thy grace, that nourisheth all things, according to the desire of them that had need: [26] That thy children, O Lord, whom thou lovest, might know, that it is not the growing of fruits that nourisheth man: but that it is thy word, which preserveth them that put their trust in thee. [27] For that which was not destroyed of the fire, being warmed with a little sunbeam, soon melted away: [28] That it might be known, that we must prevent the sun to give thee thanks, and at the dayspring pray unto thee. [29] For the hope of the unthankful shall melt away as the winter's hoar frost, and shall run away as unprofitable water.

17 [1] For great are thy judgments, and cannot be expressed: therefore unnurtured souls have erred. [2] For when unrighteous men thought to oppress the holy nation; they being shut up in their houses, the prisoners of darkness, and fettered with the bonds of a long night, lay [there] exiled from the eternal providence. [3] For while they supposed to lie hid in their secret sins, they were scattered under a dark veil of forgetfulness, being horribly astonished, and troubled with [strange] appari-

tions. [4] For neither might the corner that held them keep them from fear: but noises [as of waters] falling down sounded about them, and sad visions appeared unto them with heavy countenances. [5] No power of the fire might give them light: neither could the bright flames of the stars endure to lighten that horrible night. [6] Only there appeared unto them a fire kindled of itself, very dreadful: for being much terrified, they thought the things which they saw to be worse than the sight they saw not. [7] As for the illusions of art magic, they were put down, and their vaunting in wisdom was reproved with disgrace. [8] For they that promised to drive away terrors and troubles from a sick soul, were sick themselves of fear, worthy to be laughed at. [9] For though no terrible thing did fear them; yet being scared with beasts that passed by, and hissing of serpents, [10] they died for fear, denying that they saw the air, which could of no side be avoided. [11] For wickedness, condemned by her own witness, is very timorous, and being pressed with conscience, always forecasteth grievous things. [12] For fear is nothing else but a betraying of the succours which reason offereth. [13] And the expectation from within, being less, counteth the ignorance more than the cause which bringeth the torment. [14] But they sleeping the same sleep that night, which was indeed intolerable, and which came upon them out of the bottoms of inevitable hell, [15] Were partly vexed with monstrous apparitions, and partly fainted, their heart failing them: for a sudden fear, and not looked for, came upon them. [16] So then whosoever there fell down was straitly kept, shut up in a prison without iron bars, [17] For whether he were husbandman, or shepherd, or a labourer in the field, he was overtaken, and endured that necessity, which could not be avoided: for they were all bound with one chain of darkness. [18] Whether it were a whistling wind, or a melodious noise of birds among the spreading branches, or a pleasing fall of water running violently, [19] or a terrible sound of stones cast down, or a running that could not be seen of skipping beasts, or a roaring voice of most savage wild beasts, or a rebounding echo from the hollow mountains; these things made them swoon for fear. [20] For the whole world shined with clear light, and none were hindered in their labour: [21] Over them only was spread an heavy night, an image of that darkness which should afterward receive them: but yet were they unto themselves more grievous than the darkness.

18 [1] Nevertheless thy saints had a very great light, whose voice they hearing, and not seeing their shape, because they also had not suffered the same things, they counted them happy. [2] But for that they did not hurt them now, of whom they had been wronged before, they thanked them, and besought them pardon for that they had been enemies. [3] Instead whereof thou gavest them a burning pillar of fire, both to be a guide of the unknown journey, and an harmless sun to entertain them honourably. [4] For they were worthy to be deprived of light and imprisoned in darkness, who had kept thy sons shut up, by whom the uncorrupt light of the law was to be given unto the world. [5] And when they had determined to slay the babes of the saints, one child being cast forth, and saved, to reprove them, thou tookest away the multitude of their children, and destroyedst them altogether in a mighty water. [6] Of that night were our fathers certified afore, that assuredly, knowing unto what oaths they had given credence, they might afterwards be of good cheer. [7] So of

thy people was accepted both the salvation of the righteous, and destruction of the enemies. [8] For wherewith thou didst punish our adversaries, by the same thou didst glorify us, whom thou hadst called. [9] For the righteous children of good men did sacrifice secretly, and with one consent made a holy law, that the saints should be like partakers of the same good and evil, the fathers now singing out the songs of praise. [10] But on the other side there sounded an ill according cry of the enemies, and a lamentable noise was carried abroad for children that were bewailed. [11] The master and the servant were punished after one manner; and like as the king, so suffered the common person. [12] So they all together had innumerable dead with one kind of death; neither were the living sufficient to bury them: for in one moment the noblest offspring of them was destroyed. [13] For whereas they would not believe any thing by reason of the enchantments; upon the destruction of the firstborn, they acknowledged this people to be the sons of God. [14] For while all things were in quiet silence, and that night was in the midst of her swift course, [15] thine Almighty word leaped down from heaven out of thy royal throne, as a fierce man of war into the midst of a land of destruction, [16] and brought thine unfeigned commandment as a sharp sword, and standing up filled all things with death; and it touched the heaven, but it stood upon the earth. [17] Then suddenly visions of horrible dreams troubled them sore, and terrors came upon them unlooked for. [18] And one thrown here, and another there, half dead, shewed the cause of his death. [19] For the dreams that troubled them did foreshew this, lest they should perish, and not know why they were afflicted. [20] Yea, the tasting of death touched the righteous also, and there was a destruction of the multitude in the wilderness: but the wrath endured not long. [21] For then the blameless man made haste, and stood forth to defend them; and bringing the shield of his proper ministry, even prayer, and the propitiation of incense, set himself against the wrath, and so brought the calamity to an end, declaring that he was thy servant. [22] So he overcame the destroyer, not with strength of body, nor force of arms, but with a word subdued he him that punished, alleging the oaths and covenants made with the fathers. [23] For when the dead were now fallen down by heaps, one upon another, standing between, he stayed the wrath, and parted the way to the living. [24] For in the long garment was the whole world, and in the four rows of the stones was the glory of the fathers graven, and thy Majesty upon the diadem of his head. [25] Unto these the destroyer gave place, and was afraid of them: for it was enough that they only tasted of the wrath.

19 [1] As for the ungodly, wrath came upon them without mercy unto the end: for he knew before what they would do; [2] how that having given them leave to depart, and sent them hastily away, they would repent and pursue them. [3] For whilst they were yet mourning and making lamentation at the graves of the dead, they added another foolish device, and pursued them as fugitives, whom they had intreated to be gone. [4] For the destiny, whereof they were worthy, drew them unto this end, and made them forget the things that had already happened, that they might fulfil the punishment which was wanting to their torments: [5] And that thy people might pass a wonderful way: but they might find a strange death. [6] For the whole creature in his proper kind was fashioned again anew, serving the peculiar

commandments that were given unto them, that thy children might be kept without hurt: [7] As namely, a cloud shadowing the camp; and where water stood before, dry land appeared; and out of the Red Sea a way without impediment; and out of the violent stream a green field: [8] Wherethrough all the people went that were defended with thy hand, seeing thy marvellous strange wonders. [9] For they went at large like horses, and leaped like lambs, praising thee, O Lord, who hadst delivered them. [10] For they were yet mindful of the things that were done while they sojourned in the strange land, how the ground brought forth flies instead of cattle, and how the river cast up a multitude of frogs instead of fishes. [11] But afterwards they saw a new generation of fowls, when, being led with their appetite, they asked delicate meats. [12] For quails came up unto them from the sea for their contentment. [13] And punishments came upon the sinners, not without former signs by the force of thunders: for they suffered justly according to their own wickedness, insomuch as they used a more hard and hateful behaviour toward strangers. [14] For the Sodomites did not receive those, whom they knew not when they came: but these brought friends into bondage, that had well deserved of them. [15] And not only so, but peradventure some respect shall be had of those, because they used strangers not friendly: [16] But these very grievously afflicted them, whom they had received with feastings, and were already made partakers of the same laws with them. [17] Therefore even with blindness were these stricken, as those were at the doors of the righteous man: when, being compassed about with horrible great darkness, every one sought the passage of his own doors. [18] For the elements were changed in themselves by a kind of harmony, like as in a psaltery, notes change the name of the tune, and yet are always sounds; which may well be perceived by the sight of the things that have been done. [19] For earthly things were turned into watery, and the things that before swam in the water, now went upon the ground. [20] The fire had power in the water, forgetting his own virtue: and the water forgat his own quenching nature. [21] On the other side, the flames wasted not the flesh of the corruptible living things, though they walked therein; neither melted they the icy kind of heavenly meat that was of nature apt to melt. [22] For in all things, O Lord, thou didst magnify thy people, and glorify them, neither didst thou lightly regard them: but didst assist them in every time and place.